Better Homes and Gardens®

Oriental
COOK BOOK

On the cover: Taste-tempting *Beef and Vegetable Stir-Fry* is especially delicious served over *Deep-Fried Rice Sticks*. Garnish soy sauce with a small green onion brush. (See recipe, page 13.)

Above: Enjoy a magnificent banquet—clockwise from top: *Pork-Shrimp Meatball Soup, Tea Leaf Eggs, Sweet-Sour Glazed Riblets, Stir-Fried Pea Pods, and Grand Old Man* (see index for pages).

CONTENTS

The chances are good that if you had to choose your favorite Oriental dish, you'd name one that's classified as a main dish. That's because the vast majority of all Oriental foods are main dishes. For the same foodstuff, the differences in taste, texture, and even color and appearance come largely from the cooking technique used to prepare it. That's why a steamed chicken dish looks and tastes very different from stir-fried chicken.

The first 77 pages of the *Better Homes and Gardens Oriental Cook Book* are devoted to detailing the techniques of Oriental cookery—stir-frying, frying, firepot cooking, simmering, steaming, grilling, and roasting. Each of these sections opens with how-to illustrations accompanied by a detailed recipe to lead you step-by-step through the Oriental method of preparation. Start first with these lessons and you'll quickly become adept at stir-frying and all the other techniques.

Complementing the main part of the book are mini-chapters packed with information about salads and vegetables, noodles, rice, sauces, desserts, tea, ingredients, and menu planning. And throughout, Oriental recipes of other than Chinese influence are denoted as either Japanese or Korean.

Cooking Oriental the American Way

Certainly the most popular of all the Oriental cooking methods is stir-frying. This section features many of the traditional dishes such as *Sukiyaki* and *Chicken with Walnuts*—plus an almost limitless combination of pork, chicken, beef, seafood, and vegetable stir-fries.

Stir-Fried Main Dishes and Vegetables

In this section there's a wide variety of *deep- and shallow-fat* fried recipes with helpful cooking tips. The recipes range from the familiar wontons, egg foo yung, and *Tempura* to the impressive *Sweet and Pungent Spareribs* and spicy-hot Szechwan deep-fried fish.

Wontons, Tempura, and Other Fried Favorites

Firepot is an elegant one-dish meal that lets everyone select and cook their own food in a pot of simmering chicken broth. Savory recipes for hearty soups and delicately seasoned appetizer soups are also included, along with a host of simmered main dishes.

Firepot, Soups, and Simmered Specialties

For centuries, steaming has been an important part of the Oriental cuisine, adding both interest and variety to any meal. Steamed dumplings, *Pork-Filled Buns,* a spinach custard, *Eight-Precious Pudding,* or other main dishes and vegetables are all excellent choices.

Steaming Everything from Appetizers to Desserts

Not only did the Orientals invent the hibachi for grilling, they also developed some great-tasting oven dishes. Enjoy the tantalizing aroma of *Skewered Beef and Onion* and *Oven Barbecued Pork.*

Grilling and Roasting Meats

These recipes include a dish combining a variety of Oriental vegetables, a bean sprout and cucumber salad, and broccoli served with a soy dressing.

Salads and Vegetables

Here's a collection of tasty Oriental noodle dishes that adds interest to any menu. Included are fried noodles with vegetables, rice sticks, and deep-fried noodles.

Noodles

Orientals prepare rice in many different ways. It's served chilled in *Sushi with Smoked Fish,* fried with leftover meats, or cooked plain for an accompaniment.

Rice

When cooking Oriental, tasty sauces are an important part of the total flavor. *Sweet and Sour Sauce, Oyster Sauce,* and *Chinese Mustard* are all here.

Sauces

Finish off an Oriental meal with *Chilled Fruit Toss,* fresh pineapple, tangerines, or *Fortune Cookies.* Look to this section for recipes and serving ideas.

Desserts

Directions are given for brewing loose tea leaves, plus recipes for *Five-Spice Tea* and *Ginger-Honey Tea.* There's also information on how to serve sake.

Teas and Beverages

Here, in a labeled photograph, are most of the Oriental ingredients you'll need to prepare any recipe in this book. It's a useful guide for identifying each food item.

Oriental Ingredients

The information and cooking tips given here will help you plan and prepare a traditional Oriental meal with great success. A few sample menus are also included.

Menu Planning

Index

Better Homes and Gardens TEST KITCHEN ®

Our seal assures you that every recipe in the *Oriental Cook Book* is endorsed by the Better Homes and Gardens Test Kitchen. Each recipe is tested for family appeal, practicality, and deliciousness.

BETTER HOMES AND GARDENS® BOOKS

Editorial Director: Don Dooley
Executive Editor: Gerald Knox
Art Director: Ernest Shelton
Assistant Art Director: Randall Yontz
Production and Copy Editor: David Kirchner
Food Editor: Doris Eby
Oriental Cook Book Editors:
Sharyl Heiken, Senior Associate Food Editor
Sandra Granseth, Senior Food Editor
Senior Food Editor: Elizabeth Strait
Associate Food Editors: Diane Nelson,
Flora Szatkowski, and Patricia Teberg
Oriental Cook Book Designer:
Faith Berven
Graphic Designers: Richard Lewis,
Harijs Priekulis, and Sheryl Veenschoten
Consultants: Chu-Yen and Pansy Luke

Stir-Frying Main Dishes and Vegetables

Stir-Fried Shrimp with Vegetables

2 medium carrots
1 cup fresh mushrooms
1 pound fresh *or* frozen shrimp in shells
½ cup Homemade Chicken Broth (see recipe, page 54)
1 tablespoon cornstarch
¼ cup soy sauce
2 tablespoons cooking oil

1 clove garlic, minced
1 teaspoon grated gingerroot
1 cup thinly sliced cauliflower
2 cups chopped bok choy
1 cup fresh pea pods *or* 1 6-ounce package frozen pea pods, thawed
1 cup fresh bean sprouts *or* ½ of a 16-ounce can bean sprouts

Using sharp cleaver as shown, thinly slice carrots and mushrooms. Thaw shrimp, if frozen. Shell and devein shrimp (see sketch, page 43). Halve shrimp lengthwise. Blend chicken broth into cornstarch; stir in soy sauce and set aside.

Preheat wok or large skillet over high heat; add oil. Stir-fry garlic and gingerroot in hot oil for 30 seconds. Add cauliflower and carrots (see sketch); stir-fry 3 minutes. Add bok choy, pea pods, mushrooms, and bean sprouts; stir-fry 2 minutes more or till vegetables are crisp-tender (be sure to keep heat high throughout). Remove vegetables to bowl. (Add more oil to wok or skillet, if necessary.) Add shrimp to *hot* wok or skillet; stir-fry 7 to 8 minutes or till shrimp are done. Push shrimp away from center of wok or skillet.

Stir chicken broth mixture and add to center of wok or skillet, as shown. Cook and stir till thickened and bubbly. Stir in vegetables; cover and cook 1 minute. Serve at once. Serves 4.

Grasp cleaver blade between thumb and index finger and wrap remaining three fingers around handle as shown. With other hand, hold food with fingertips curled under and knuckles against blade, as shown (see tip, page 8).

To stir-fry, use a long-handled spoon or spatula to frequently lift and turn the food with a folding motion. Be sure to keep heat set on high so food cooks quickly (see tip box, page 18).

Push food away from center of wok or skillet. Then, add thickening mixture, as shown. Let bubble slightly before stirring into food.

Oriental Shrimp

1 **pound fresh** *or* **frozen large shrimp in shells**
2 **tablespoons cooking oil**
2 **tablespoons catsup**
2 **tablespoons worcestershire sauce**
2 **teaspoons soy sauce**
2 **teaspoons dry sherry** *or* **cognac**
1 **teaspoon sugar**
6 **drops bottled hot pepper sauce**

Thaw shrimp, if frozen. Peel and devein shrimp (see sketch, page 43). Preheat a wok or large skillet over high heat; add cooking oil. Stir-fry shrimp in hot oil 7 to 8 minutes or till shrimp are done. Remove shrimp; drain off oil from wok or skillet. Add catsup, worcestershire, soy sauce, sherry or cognac, sugar, and hot pepper sauce to wok or skillet; heat to boiling. Return shrimp to wok or skillet; cover and cook for 30 seconds. Serve at once. Makes 4 servings.

Stir-Fried Shrimp with Pineapple

1 **pound fresh** *or* **frozen shrimp in shells**
1 **8¼-ounce can pineapple chunks**
2 **teaspoons cornstarch**
3 **tablespoons soy sauce**
2 **tablespoons cooking oil**
1 **teaspoon grated gingerroot**
8 **green onions, bias-sliced into 1½-inch lengths**
1 **8-ounce can water chestnuts, drained and sliced**

Thaw shrimp, if frozen. Shell and devein shrimp (see sketch, page 43). Halve shrimp lengthwise. Drain pineapple, reserving liquid. Blend reserved pineapple liquid into cornstarch; stir in soy sauce and set aside.

Preheat wok or large skillet over high heat; add oil. Stir-fry gingerroot in hot oil for 30 seconds. Add green onion and stir-fry 1 minute. Add water chestnuts; stir-fry 1 minute more. Remove green onion and water chestnuts. (Add more oil, if necessary.) Add shrimp to *hot* wok or skillet; stir-fry 7 to 8 minutes or till shrimp are done. Stir soy sauce mixture and stir into shrimp in wok or skillet. Cook and stir till thickened and bubbly. Stir in pineapple, green onion, and water chestnuts; cover and cook 2 minutes more. Serve at once. Makes 4 servings.

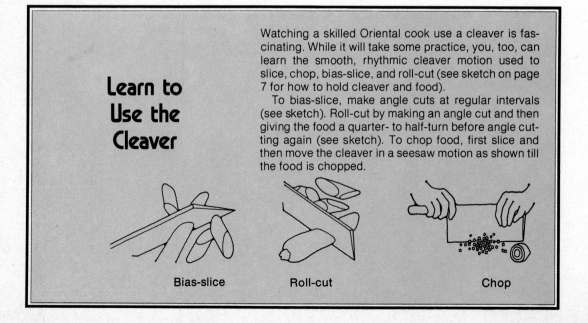

Learn to Use the Cleaver

Watching a skilled Oriental cook use a cleaver is fascinating. While it will take some practice, you, too, can learn the smooth, rhythmic cleaver motion used to slice, chop, bias-slice, and roll-cut (see sketch on page 7 for how to hold cleaver and food).

To bias-slice, make angle cuts at regular intervals (see sketch). Roll-cut by making an angle cut and then giving the food a quarter- to half-turn before angle cutting again (see sketch). To chop food, first slice and then move the cleaver in a seesaw motion as shown till the food is chopped.

Bias-slice   Roll-cut   Chop

Peppery Crab with Asparagus

½ **pound fresh crab meat, cooked and shelled** *or* **1 6-ounce package frozen cooked crab meat**
⅓ **cup Homemade Chicken Broth (see recipe, page 54)**
2 **teaspoons cornstarch**
2 **tablespoons dry sherry**
1 **tablespoon soy sauce**
1 **teaspoon sugar**
⅛ **teaspoon crushed red pepper**
1 **teaspoon grated gingerroot**
2 **tablespoons cooking oil**
¾ **pound asparagus, bias-sliced into 1-inch lengths (2 cups)**
¼ **cup sliced green onion**

Thaw crab, if frozen. Cut crab into bite-size pieces. Blend chicken broth into cornstarch; stir in sherry, soy sauce, sugar, and crushed red pepper. Set aside.

Preheat wok or large skillet over high heat; add oil. Stir-fry gingerroot in hot oil for 30 seconds. Add asparagus; stir-fry 3 minutes or till crisp-tender. Add green onion; stir-fry 1 minute more. Remove asparagus and green onion. (Add more oil, if necessary.) Add crab to *hot* wok or skillet; stir-fry 1½ minutes. Stir chicken broth mixture; stir into crab. Cook and stir till thickened and bubbly. Stir in asparagus and green onion; cover and cook 2 to 3 minutes. Serve at once. Makes 3 or 4 servings.

Beef-Cucumber Stir-Fry

1 **pound beef top round steak**
2 **medium cucumbers**
¼ **teaspoon instant beef bouillon granules**
¼ **cup boiling water**
3 **tablespoons soy sauce**
2 **tablespoons dry sherry**
2 **teaspoons cornstarch**
2 **tablespoons cooking oil**
1 **clove garlic, minced**
8 **green onions, bias-sliced into 1-inch lengths**
½ **cup coarsely shredded carrot**

Partially freeze beef. Slice beef very thinly across the grain into bite-size strips. Peel cucumbers; cut cucumbers into 1-inch-thick slices and seed. Dissolve bouillon in boiling water. Blend soy sauce and sherry into cornstarch; stir into beef bouillon. Set aside. Preheat wok or large skillet over high heat; add oil. Stir-fry garlic in hot oil for 30 seconds. Add green onions and carrot and stir-fry 1½ minutes. Add cucumbers and stir-fry 30 seconds more. Remove onions, carrot, and cucumbers. (Add more oil, if necessary.) Add *half* the beef to *hot* wok or skillet; stir-fry 2 to 3 minutes or till browned. Remove beef. Stir-fry remaining beef 2 to 3 minutes. Return all meat to wok or skillet. Stir bouillon mixture and stir into beef. Cook and stir till thickened and bubbly. Stir in onions, cucumbers, and carrot; cover and cook 2 minutes. Makes 4 to 6 servings.

Beef Strips with Oyster Sauce

1 **pound beef top round steak**
½ **cup cold water**
1 **tablespoon cornstarch**
2 **tablespoons Oyster Sauce (see recipe, page 85)**
2 **tablespoons dry sherry**
1 **tablespoon soy sauce**
½ **teaspoon sugar**
2 **tablespoons cooking oil**
1 **large onion, thinly sliced and separated into rings**
Hot cooked rice

Partially freeze beef. Slice beef thinly across the grain into bite-size strips. For marinade, blend water into cornstarch; stir in oyster sauce, sherry, soy sauce, and sugar; mix well. Add beef; let stand 30 minutes at room temperature. Drain meat, reserving marinade; set aside.

Preheat wok or large skillet over high heat; add the oil. Stir-fry onion in hot oil about 3 minutes or till crisp-tender. Remove onion. (Add more oil, if necessary.) Add *half* the beef to *hot* wok or skillet; stir-fry 2 to 3 minutes or till browned. Remove beef. Stir-fry remaining beef 2 to 3 minutes. Return all meat to wok or skillet.

Stir reserved marinade and stir into beef. Cook and stir till thickened and bubbly. Stir in onion; cover and cook 1 minute. Serve at once over hot cooked rice. Makes 4 servings.

Sukiyaki

½   **pound beef top round steak**
½   **teaspoon instant beef bouillon
      granules**
¼   **cup boiling water**
3   **tablespoons soy sauce**
1   **tablespoon sugar**
2   **tablespoons cooking oil**
3   **cups thinly sliced bok choy**
1   **cup green onions, bias-sliced
      into 1-inch lengths**
½   **cup bias-sliced celery**
8   **ounces fresh tofu (bean curd),
      cubed**
1   **cup fresh bean sprouts *or* ½ of a
      16-ounce can bean sprouts,
      drained**
½   **of an 8-ounce can bamboo
      shoots, drained**
½   **cup thinly sliced fresh
      mushrooms**
½   **of an 8-ounce can water
      chestnuts, drained and thinly
      sliced**

Partially freeze beef. Slice beef very thinly across the grain into bite-size strips. Dissolve beef bouillon granules in boiling water; add soy sauce and sugar.

Preheat a wok or large skillet over high heat; add oil. Add bok choy, green onions, and celery; stir-fry 2 minutes. Remove bok choy, green onions, and celery. Add tofu, bean sprouts, bamboo shoots, mushrooms, and water chestnuts; stir-fry 1 minute. Remove vegetables. (Add more oil, if necessary.) Add the beef to *hot* wok or skillet; stir-fry 2 minutes or till meat is just browned. Stir beef bouillon mixture; stir into beef. Cook and stir till bubbly. Stir in vegetables. Cover and cook for 1 minute or till just heated through. Serve at once. Makes 2 or 3 servings.

Spicy Beef and Asparagus

1   **pound beef top round steak**
1   **egg white**
1   **tablespoon cornstarch**
1   **teaspoon dry sherry**
½   **teaspoon salt**
½   **teaspoon pepper
      Several dashes bottled hot
      pepper sauce**
1   **tablespoon soy sauce**
1   **tablespoon catsup**
1   **teaspoon red wine vinegar**
½   **teaspoon sugar**
2   **tablespoons cooking oil**
1   **clove garlic, minced**
¾   **pound fresh asparagus, cut in
      1-inch lengths (2 cups) *or* 1
      10-ounce package frozen cut
      asparagus, thawed**
1   **cup thinly sliced fresh
      mushrooms *or* 1 4½-ounce can
      sliced mushrooms, drained**
¼   **cup thinly sliced green onion**

Partially freeze meat; thinly slice meat across the grain into bite-size strips. In bowl combine beef strips, egg white, cornstarch, dry sherry, salt, pepper, and hot pepper sauce. By hand, work the seasonings into the meat. Combine soy sauce, catsup, vinegar, and sugar; set aside.

Preheat wok or large skillet over high heat; add oil. Stir-fry garlic in hot oil for 30 seconds. Add asparagus, mushrooms, and green onion; stir-fry about 6 minutes or till asparagus is crisp-tender (less time required if using frozen asparagus). Remove asparagus and mushrooms. (Add oil, if necessary.) Add *half* the meat to *hot* wok or skillet; stir-fry 2 to 3 minutes or till meat is just browned. Remove meat. Stir-fry remaining meat 2 to 3 minutes. Return meat to wok or skillet. Stir soy sauce mixture; stir into beef. Cook and stir till bubbly. Stir in vegetables. Cover and cook for 1 minute or till just heated through. Serve at once. Makes 4 to 6 servings.

Beef strips and a variety of Oriental vegetables are stir-fried to perfection in the Japanese favorite, *Sukiyaki.*

Stir-Fried Tomato and Beef

1 **pound beef top round steak**
½ **teaspoon instant beef bouillon granules**
⅓ **cup boiling water**
¼ **cup soy sauce**
1 **tablespoon cornstarch**
2 **tablespoons cooking oil**
1 **teaspoon grated gingerroot**
6 **green onions, bias-sliced into 1-inch lengths**
½ **cup shredded carrot**
1 **large green pepper, cut in narrow strips**
½ **cup thinly sliced celery**
2 **tomatoes, cut in wedges**

Partially freeze beef; slice thinly across the grain into bite-size strips. Dissolve bouillon granules in water. Blend soy sauce into cornstarch; stir in bouillon. Set aside.

Preheat a wok or large skillet over high heat; add cooking oil. Stir-fry gingerroot in hot oil 30 seconds. Add green onions and carrot; stir-fry 2 minutes. Remove green onions and carrot. Add green pepper and celery; stir-fry 2 minutes. Remove green pepper and celery. (Add more oil, if necessary.) Add *half* the beef to *hot* wok or skillet; stir-fry 2 to 3 minutes or till browned. Remove beef. Stir-fry remaining beef 2 to 3 minutes. Return all meat to wok or skillet. Stir soy sauce mixture and stir into beef. Cook and stir till thickened and bubbly. Stir in green onions, carrot, green pepper, celery, and tomatoes; cover and cook for 1 minute. Serve at once. Makes 4 servings.

Beef with Peanuts

1 **pound beef top round steak**
1 **teaspoon instant beef bouillon granules**
½ **cup boiling water**
2 **tablespoons soy sauce**
1 **tablespoon cornstarch**
2 **tablespoons cooking oil**
½ **cup raw peanuts**
½ **cup chopped onion**
1 **clove garlic, minced**
4 **cups chopped bok choy**
2 **cups fresh bean sprouts *or* 1 16-ounce can bean sprouts, drained**

Partially freeze beef; slice thinly across the grain into bite-size strips. Dissolve bouillon granules in water. Blend soy sauce into cornstarch; stir in bouillon. Set aside.

Preheat a wok or large skillet over high heat; add cooking oil. Stir-fry peanuts over high heat in hot oil for 2 to 3 minutes or till lightly browned. Remove peanuts. Add onion and garlic; stir-fry 1 minute. Add bok choy; stir-fry 1 minute more. Add bean sprouts; stir-fry 1 minute more. Remove vegetables. (Add more oil, if necessary.) Add *half* the beef to *hot* wok or skillet; stir-fry 2 to 3 minutes or till browned. Remove beef. Stir-fry remaining beef 2 to 3 minutes. Return all meat to wok or skillet. Stir soy mixture and stir into beef. Cook and stir till thickened and bubbly. Stir in vegetables; cover and cook 1 minute. Stir in peanuts. Serve at once. Serves 6.

Beef with Pea Pods

1 **pound beef top round steak**
2 **teaspoons cornstarch**
1 **teaspoon sugar**
2 **tablespoons soy sauce**
2 **tablespoons Oyster Sauce (optional) (see recipe, page 85)**
2 **tablespoons cooking oil**
1 **clove garlic, minced**
½ **teaspoon grated gingerroot**
2 **cups fresh pea pods *or* 1 6-ounce package frozen pea pods, thawed**
½ **of 8-ounce can (½ cup) water chestnuts, drained and thinly sliced**

Partially freeze beef; slice thinly across the grain into bite-size strips. In small bowl mix cornstarch, sugar, ½ teaspoon *salt,* and ⅛ teaspoon *pepper.* Blend in soy sauce; oyster sauce, if desired; and ¼ cup *water.* Set aside.

Preheat a wok or large skillet over high heat; add cooking oil. Stir-fry garlic and gingerroot in hot oil for 30 seconds. Add pea pods and water chestnuts to wok. Stir-fry about 1 minute. Remove pea pods and water chestnuts from wok. (Add more oil if necessary.) Add *half* the beef to *hot* wok or skillet; stir-fry 2 to 3 minutes or till browned. Remove beef. Stir-fry remaining beef 2 to 3 minutes. Return all meat to wok or skillet. Stir soy mixture and stir into beef. Cook and stir till mixture is thickened and bubbly. Stir in pea pods and water chestnuts; cover and cook 1 minute. Serve at once. Makes 4 servings.

Beef and Vegetables with Oyster Sauce

1 pound beef top round steak
2 tablespoons soy sauce
1 tablespoon cornstarch
¼ cup Oyster Sauce (see recipe, page 85)
2 tablespoons dry sherry
2 tablespoons cooking oil
1 clove garlic, minced
1 cup celery bias-sliced into ½-inch lengths
1 10-ounce package frozen peas, thawed
3 cups chopped bok choy

Partially freeze beef; slice very thinly across the grain into bite-size strips. Blend soy sauce into cornstarch; stir in oyster sauce and dry sherry. Set aside.

Preheat a wok or large skillet over high heat; add oil. Stir-fry garlic in hot oil for 30 seconds. Add celery; stir-fry 1 minute. Add peas; stir-fry 1 minute more. Remove celery and peas. Add bok choy; stir-fry 1 minute. Remove bok choy. (Add more oil, if necessary.) Add *half* the beef to *hot* wok or skillet; stir-fry 2 to 3 minutes or till browned. Remove beef. Stir-fry remaining beef 2 to 3 minutes. Return all meat to wok or skillet. Stir oyster sauce mixture; stir into beef. Cook and stir till thickened and bubbly. Stir in vegetables; cover and cook 2 minutes. Serve at once. Serves 4 to 6.

Beef and Vegetable Stir-Fry *(pictured on the cover)*

1 pound beef top round steak
1½ cups broccoli cut into 1-inch pieces
3 medium carrots, bias-sliced
1 teaspoon cornstarch
1 teaspoon salt
½ teaspoon sugar
2 tablespoons soy sauce
2 tablespoons dry sherry
2 tablespoons cooking oil
1 medium onion, cut in thin wedges
½ of a 10-ounce package (1 cup) frozen peas, thawed
½ cup water chestnuts, drained and thinly sliced
½ cup bamboo shoots, halved lengthwise
Deep-Fried Rice Sticks *or* hot cooked rice

Partially freeze beef; slice very thinly across the grain into bite-size strips. Cook broccoli and carrots, covered, in boiling salted water 2 minutes; drain. Mix cornstarch, salt, and sugar; blend in soy sauce and sherry. Set aside.

Preheat a wok or large skillet over high heat; add oil. Stir-fry broccoli, carrots, and onion in hot oil for 2 minutes or till crisp-tender. Remove from wok. (Add more oil, if necessary.) Add *half* the beef to *hot* wok or skillet; stir-fry 2 to 3 minutes or till browned. Remove beef. Stir-fry remaining beef 2 to 3 minutes. Return all meat to wok or skillet. Add peas, water chestnuts, and bamboo shoots. Stir soy mixture; stir into wok. Cook and stir till thickened and bubbly. Return broccoli, carrots, and onion to wok; cover and cook 1 minute more. Serve atop Deep-Fried Rice Sticks or with rice. Serves 4 to 6.

Deep-Fried Rice Sticks: Fry 2 ounces *unsoaked rice sticks,* a few at a time, in deep hot *cooking oil* (375°) about 5 seconds or just till sticks puff and rise to top. Remove; drain on paper toweling. Keep warm in oven. (Store any uncooked rice sticks in a tightly closed plastic bag.)

Caring for Your Wok

A new wok must be seasoned before using. First scrub your wok with cleanser or scouring pads to remove the rust-resistant coating applied during manufacturing. Then wipe wok and heat it on the range to dry.

Season the wok by heating two tablespoons cooking oil in the pan. Tilt and rotate the wok till the entire inner surface is coated. Cool the wok and dry it with paper toweling.

After each use soak your wok in hot water. Then use a bamboo brush or sponge to clean it. Rinse, hand-dry, and heat the wok on the range to dry excess water. Then rub a teaspoon of cooking oil over the inner surface.

Pork and Asparagus

1 **pound boneless pork**
2 **tablespoons soy sauce**
2 **teaspoons cornstarch**
2 **tablespoons sweet bean sauce**
2 **tablespoons cooking oil**
1 **clove garlic, minced**
2 **cups fresh asparagus bias-sliced into 1-inch lengths**
½ **cup sliced water chestnuts**

Partially freeze pork; slice thinly into bite-size strips. Blend soy into cornstarch; stir in bean sauce. Set aside.

Preheat a wok or large skillet over high heat; add cooking oil. Stir-fry garlic in hot oil for 30 seconds. Add asparagus; stir-fry 2 minutes. Add water chestnuts; stir-fry 1 minute more. Remove vegetables. (Add more oil, if necessary.) Add half the pork to *hot* wok or skillet; stir-fry 2 to 3 minutes. Remove pork. Stir-fry remaining pork 2 to 3 minutes. Return all meat to wok or skillet. Stir soy mixture; stir into pork. Cook and stir till thickened and bubbly. Stir in asparagus and water chestnuts; cover and cook for 1 minute. Serve at once. Makes 4 servings.

Stir-Fried Pork with Tofu

1 **pound boneless pork**
4 **dried mushrooms**
2 **tablespoons dried lily buds**
¼ **cup soy sauce**
2 **teaspoons cornstarch**
2 **tablespoons dry sherry**
8 **ounces fresh tofu (bean curd)**
3 **tablespoons cooking oil**
1 **teaspoon grated gingerroot**
1 **clove garlic, minced**
4 **cups chopped Chinese cabbage**
1 **cup thinly sliced celery**

Partially freeze pork; slice thinly into bite-size strips. Soak mushrooms and lily buds in warm water to cover for 30 minutes; squeeze to drain well. Chop mushrooms, discarding stems. Cut lily buds in 1-inch lengths. Blend soy sauce into cornstarch; stir in dry sherry. Set aside. Place tofu in double thickness of cheesecloth or paper toweling. Press gently to extract as much moisture as possible. Cube tofu.

Preheat a wok or large skillet over high heat; add cooking oil. Stir-fry tofu in hot oil for 3 minutes, turning several times. Remove tofu. Add gingerroot and garlic to *hot* wok; stir-fry 30 seconds. Add mushrooms and lily buds; stir-fry 1 minute. Remove mushrooms and lily buds. Add Chinese cabbage and celery; stir-fry 3 minutes. Remove celery and cabbage. (Add more oil, if necessary.) Add *half* the pork to *hot* wok or skillet; stir-fry 2 to 3 minutes. Remove pork. Stir-fry remaining pork 2 to 3 minutes. Return all meat to wok or skillet. Stir soy sauce mixture; stir into pork. Cook and stir till thickened and bubbly. Stir in mushrooms, lily buds, celery, and Chinese cabbage; cover and cook 1 minute. *Gently* stir in tofu. Serve at once. Serves 6.

Mandarin Twice-Cooked Pork

1 **pound boneless pork shoulder**
½ **cup water**
3 **tablespoons dry sherry**
2 **tablespoons sliced green onion**
1 **teaspoon grated gingerroot**
2 **tablespoons sweet bean sauce**
2 **tablespoons hot bean sauce**
2 **tablespoons soy sauce**
1 **tablespoon water**
2 **teaspoons sugar**
1 **tablespoon cooking oil**
3 **medium green peppers, cut into ¾-inch pieces**
2 **cloves garlic, minced**

In wok or large skillet combine pork, the ½ cup water, sherry, green onion, and gingerroot. Cover; simmer 25 to 30 minutes. Drain; cool. Discard liquid. Slice meat very thinly into bite-size pieces. Combine sweet bean sauce, hot bean sauce, soy sauce, the 1 tablespoon water, and sugar. Set aside.

Preheat a wok or large skillet over high heat; add cooking oil. Stir-fry green peppers and garlic in hot oil for 2 to 3 minutes. Remove green peppers. (Add more oil, if necessary.) Add the pork to *hot* wok or skillet; stir-fry for 2 to 3 minutes. Stir soy mixture; stir into pork. Cook and stir till bubbly. Stir in green peppers; cover and cook for 1 minute. Serve at once. Makes 4 servings.

Stir-Fried Pork with Spinach

1½ **pounds boneless pork**
3 **tablespoons soy sauce**
¼ **teaspoon Homemade Five Spice Powder (see recipe, page 31)**
¼ **cup Homemade Chicken Broth (see recipe, page 54)**
2 **teaspoons cornstarch**
2 **tablespoons cooking oil**
1 **teaspoon grated gingerroot**
6 **cups small fresh spinach leaves**

Partially freeze pork; slice thinly into bite-size strips. Combine pork, soy sauce, and five spice powder; let stand 15 minutes at room temperature. Blend chicken broth into cornstarch. Set aside.

Preheat a wok or large skillet over high heat; add cooking oil. Stir-fry gingerroot in hot oil for 30 seconds. Add spinach to wok; stir-fry 2 minutes. Remove spinach. (Add more oil, if necessary.) Add *half* the pork to *hot* wok or skillet; stir-fry 2 to 3 minutes or till browned. Remove pork. Stir-fry remaining pork 2 to 3 minutes. Return all pork to wok or skillet. Stir broth mixture and stir into pork. Cook and stir till thickened and bubbly. Stir in spinach; cover and cook 1 minute. Serve at once. Serves 6.

Pork-Cashew Stir-Fry

1½ **pounds boneless pork**
2 **tablespoons soy sauce**
¼ **teaspoon Homemade Five Spice Powder (see recipe, page 31)**
¼ **cup cold water**
2 **teaspoons cornstarch**
¼ **cup soy sauce**
2 **tablespoons cooking oil**
1 **teaspoon grated gingerroot**
6 **green onions, bias-sliced into 1-inch lengths**
1 **cup cashews**

Partially freeze pork; slice thinly into bite-size strips. Combine pork, the 2 tablespoons soy sauce, and five spice powder; let stand 15 minutes at room temperature. In small bowl blend cold water into cornstarch; stir in the ¼ cup soy sauce. Set aside.

Preheat a wok or large skillet over high heat; add cooking oil. Stir-fry gingerroot in hot oil 30 seconds. Add green onions; stir-fry 1 minute. Add cashews; stir-fry 1 to 2 minutes or till nuts are just golden. Remove cashews and green onions. (Add more oil, if necessary.) Add *half* of the pork to *hot* wok or skillet; stir-fry 2 minutes. Remove pork. Stir-fry remaining pork 2 minutes. Return all pork to wok or skillet. Stir soy mixture; stir into pork. Cook and stir till thickened and bubbly. Stir in green onions and cashews; cover and cook 1 minute. Serve at once. Makes 6 servings.

Peppery Pork

1 **pound boneless pork**
¼ **cup soy sauce**
2 **teaspoons cornstarch**
⅓ **cup water**
½ **teaspoon pepper *or* crushed Szechwan pepper**
2 **tablespoons cooking oil**
1 **teaspoon grated gingerroot**
1 **clove garlic, minced**
2 **cups chopped Chinese cabbage**
6 **green onions, bias-sliced into 1-inch lengths**
1 **8-ounce can bamboo shoots, drained**

Partially freeze pork; slice thinly into bite-size strips. In small bowl blend soy sauce into cornstarch; stir in water and pepper. Set aside.

Preheat a wok or large skillet over high heat; add cooking oil. Stir-fry gingerroot and garlic in hot oil for 30 seconds. Add Chinese cabbage; stir-fry 2 minutes. Add green onions and bamboo shoots; stir-fry 1 minute more. Remove vegetables. (Add more oil, if necessary.) Add *half* the pork to *hot* wok or skillet; stir-fry 2 minutes. Remove pork. Stir-fry remaining pork 2 to 3 minutes. Return all meat to wok or skillet. Stir soy mixture; stir into pork. Cook and stir till thickened and bubbly. Stir in Chinese cabbage, green onions, and bamboo shoots; cover and cook 1 minute. Serve at once. Makes 4 servings.

Pork with Celery and Tomatoes

½ **pound boneless pork**
1 **teaspoon instant beef bouillon granules**
⅓ **cup boiling water**
1 **tablespoon soy sauce**
1 **tablespoon cornstarch**
¼ **teaspoon salt**
2 **tablespoons cooking oil**
1 **clove garlic, minced**
1 **teaspoon grated gingerroot**
2 **cups bias-sliced celery**
4 **green onions, bias-sliced into 1-inch lengths**
2 **medium tomatoes, cut in thin wedges**

Partially freeze pork; slice thinly into bite-size strips. Dissolve beef bouillon granules in boiling water. Blend soy sauce into cornstarch; stir in bouillon and salt. Set aside.

Preheat a wok or large skillet over high heat; add cooking oil. Stir-fry garlic and gingerroot in hot oil 30 seconds. Add celery and green onions; stir-fry 2 minutes or till crisp-tender. Remove celery and green onions. (Add more oil, if necessary.) Add pork to *hot* wok or skillet; stir-fry 3 minutes or till just browned. Stir bouillon mixture; stir into pork. Cook and stir till thickened and bubbly. Add celery, green onions, and tomatoes; cover and heat 1 minute. Serve at once. Makes 2 or 3 servings.

Stir-Fried Pork with Mandarin Oranges

1 **pound boneless pork**
2 **tablespoons soy sauce**
2 **teaspoons cornstarch**
1 **teaspoon grated orange peel**
½ **cup orange juice**
2 **tablespoons cooking oil**
1 **teaspoon grated gingerroot**
2 **cups fresh pea pods *or* 1 6-ounce package frozen pea pods, thawed**
1 **11-ounce can mandarin orange sections, drained**

Partially freeze pork; slice thinly into bite-size strips. In a small bowl blend soy sauce into cornstarch; stir in orange peel and orange juice. Set aside.

Preheat a wok or large skillet over high heat; add cooking oil. Stir-fry gingerroot in hot oil 30 seconds. Add pea pods; stir-fry 2 minutes for fresh pea pods *or* 1 minute for thawed frozen pea pods. Remove pea pods. (Add more oil, if necessary.) Add *half* of the pork to *hot* wok or skillet; stir-fry 2 to 3 minutes. Remove from wok. Stir-fry remaining pork 2 to 3 minutes. Return all pork to wok or skillet. Stir soy sauce mixture and stir into pork. Cook and stir till thickened and bubbly. Stir in pea pods; cover and cook 1 minute more. Remove from heat; stir in drained oranges. Serve at once. Makes 4 servings.

Chicken with Walnuts

1½ **pounds whole chicken breasts, skinned, split, and boned**
3 **tablespoons soy sauce**
2 **teaspoons cornstarch**
2 **tablespoons dry sherry**
1 **teaspoon grated gingerroot**
1 **teaspoon sugar**
½ **teaspoon salt**
½ **teaspoon crushed red pepper**
2 **tablespoons cooking oil**
2 **medium green peppers, cut into ¾-inch pieces**
4 **green onions, bias-sliced into 1-inch lengths**
1 **cup walnut halves**

Cut chicken into 1-inch pieces. Set aside. In small bowl blend soy sauce into cornstarch; stir in dry sherry, gingerroot, sugar, salt, and red pepper. Set aside.

Preheat a wok or large skillet over high heat; add cooking oil. Stir-fry green peppers and green onions in hot oil 2 minutes or till crisp-tender. Remove from wok. Add walnuts to wok; stir-fry 1 to 2 minutes or till just golden. Remove from wok. (Add more oil, if necessary.) Add *half* of the chicken to *hot* wok or skillet; stir-fry 2 minutes. Remove from wok. Stir-fry remaining chicken 2 minutes. Return all chicken to wok or skillet. Stir soy mixture; stir into chicken. Cook and stir till thickened and bubbly. Stir in vegetables; cover and cook 1 minute more. Serve at once. Garnish with fresh kumquats and serve with hot cooked rice, if desired. Makes 4 to 6 servings.

Your skill with chopsticks is sure to improve with the tantalizing flavor of *Chicken with Walnuts* to spur you on.

Lemon Chicken and Zucchini

1½ **pounds chicken breasts and**
    thighs
¼ **cup Homemade Chicken Broth**
    (see recipe, page 54)
1 **tablespoon cornstarch**
2 **tablespoons soy sauce**
1 **teaspoon sugar**
2 **tablespoons cooking oil**
1 **teaspoon grated gingerroot**
3½ **cups sliced zucchini**
2 **tablespoons lemon juice**
    Deep-Fried Rice Sticks (see
    recipe, page 13)

Skin, split, and bone chicken breasts. Skin and bone chicken thighs. Cut chicken into 1-inch pieces. Blend chicken broth into cornstarch; stir in soy sauce and sugar. Set aside.

Preheat a wok or large skillet over high heat; add cooking oil. Stir-fry gingerroot in hot oil for 30 seconds. Stir-fry *half* of the zucchini for 2 to 3 minutes or till crisp-tender. Remove zucchini. Stir-fry remaining zucchini 2 to 3 minutes. Remove from wok. (Add more oil, if necessary.) Add *half* the chicken to *hot* wok or skillet; stir-fry 2 minutes or till done. Remove chicken. Stir-fry remaining chicken 2 minutes. Return all chicken to wok or skillet. Stir broth mixture; stir into chicken. Cook and stir till thickened and bubbly. Add zucchini and lemon juice; cover and cook 1 minute more. Serve atop Deep-Fried Rice Sticks. Makes 4 to 6 servings.

Chicken Livers with Mushrooms

¼ **cup Homemade Chicken Broth**
    (see recipe, page 54)
2 **teaspoons cornstarch**
2 **tablespoons dry sherry**
2 **tablespoons cooking oil**
1 **clove garlic, minced**
1 **large green pepper, cut into**
    1-inch pieces
1 **onion, cut in thin wedges**
2 **cups sliced fresh mushrooms**
8 **ounces chicken livers, halved**

Blend broth into cornstarch; stir in sherry. Set aside.

Preheat a wok or large skillet over high heat; add cooking oil. Stir-fry garlic in hot oil for 30 seconds. Add green pepper and onion. Stir-fry 3 minutes. Remove green pepper and onion. Add fresh mushrooms; stir-fry 1 minute. Remove mushrooms. (Add more oil, if necessary.) Add chicken livers to *hot* wok or skillet; stir-fry 3 to 4 minutes or till just pink. Stir broth mixture; stir into chicken livers. Cook and stir till thickened and bubbly. Stir in green pepper, onion, and mushrooms; cover and cook 2 minutes more. Serve at once. Makes 4 servings.

Adjust Your Wok to Your Range

Heating your wok to the proper temperature is easy if you follow these guidelines. For *gas* ranges, place wide end of the ring stand *down* over the largest burner (see drawing, below left). Then place your wok in the stand and turn heat to highest setting. Heat the wok a few minutes. Then add cooking oil and allow it to heat a few minutes more. For *electric* ranges, place wide end of your ring stand *up* over the largest burner (see drawing, below right) and place wok inside the stand. This allows the wok to sit closer to the electric coil. Then turn heat to highest setting and proceed as for a gas range.

Gas range

Electric range

Kung Bow Chicken

½ cup dried mushrooms
1 whole large chicken breast, skinned, split, and boned
1 teaspoon cornstarch
3 tablespoons soy sauce
1 tablespoon cooking oil
1 clove garlic, minced
1 large green pepper, cut into ½-inch pieces
½ cup bamboo shoots, cut in half lengthwise
2 tablespoons chopped peanuts
¼ teaspoon crushed red pepper

Soak mushrooms in enough warm water to cover for 30 minutes; squeeze to drain well. Chop mushrooms, discarding stems. Cut chicken into bite-size pieces. Blend 1 tablespoon cold *water* into cornstarch; stir in soy sauce. Set aside.

Preheat a wok or large skillet over high heat; add cooking oil. Stir-fry garlic in hot oil 30 seconds. Add green pepper, bamboo shoots, peanuts, red pepper, and mushrooms. Stir-fry 2 minutes. Remove from wok. (Add more oil, if necessary.) Add chicken; stir-fry 2 minutes. Stir soy mixture; stir into chicken. Cook and stir till thickened and bubbly. Add green pepper, bamboo shoots, peanuts, red pepper, and mushrooms; cover and cook 1 minute. Serve at once. Makes 2 servings.

Chicken and Hot Peppers

1 8¼-ounce can pineapple slices
1½ teaspoons cornstarch
2 tablespoons soy sauce
2 whole chicken breasts, skinned, split, boned, and cut into 1-inch pieces
2 tablespoons cooking oil
1 clove garlic, minced
6 green onions, bias-sliced into 1-inch lengths
1 4-ounce can green chili peppers, rinsed, seeded, and chopped

Drain pineapple; reserve ⅓ cup syrup. Quarter pineapple slices. Blend reserved syrup into cornstarch; stir in soy sauce. Add chicken; marinate 30 minutes at room temperature. Drain chicken, reserving marinade.

Preheat a wok or large skillet over high heat; add oil. Stir-fry garlic in hot oil 30 seconds. Add green onions; stir-fry 1 minute. Add chili peppers; stir-fry 1 minute more. Remove vegetables. (Add more oil, if necessary.) Add *half* the chicken to *hot* wok or skillet; stir-fry 2 to 3 minutes. Remove chicken. Stir-fry remaining chicken 2 to 3 minutes. Return all chicken to wok. Stir marinade; stir into chicken. Cook and stir till thickened and bubbly. Add onions, peppers, and pineapple; cover and cook 1 minute. Serves 4.

Chicken and Pork Chow Mein

½ pound boneless pork shoulder*
2 cups fine egg noodles
½ cup Homemade Chicken Broth (see recipe, page 54)
1 tablespoon cornstarch
3 tablespoons soy sauce
3 tablespoons cooking oil
1 teaspoon grated gingerroot
6 green onions, bias-sliced into 1-inch lengths
3 cups chopped Chinese cabbage
1 4-ounce can sliced mushrooms, drained
1 whole large chicken breast, skinned, split, boned, and cut into 1-inch pieces

Partially freeze pork. Slice pork thinly into bite-size strips. Cook noodles according to package directions. Drain; rinse with cold water. Drain well. Blend chicken broth into cornstarch; stir in soy sauce. Set aside.

Preheat a wok or large skillet over high heat; add *2 tablespoons* of the oil. Stir-fry gingerroot in hot oil 30 seconds. Add noodles; stir-fry 6 minutes. Remove noodles; keep warm. Add *1 tablespoon* oil to wok. Add green onions; stir-fry 1 minute. Remove green onions. Add Chinese cabbage; stir-fry 2 minutes. Add mushrooms; stir-fry 1 minute more. Remove vegetables. Add chicken to *hot* wok or skillet; stir-fry 2 minutes. Remove chicken. (Add more oil, if necessary.) Add pork; stir-fry 2 minutes. Add chicken to wok. Stir soy mixture; stir into meat. Cook and stir till thickened and bubbly. Add the green onions, Chinese cabbage, and mushrooms; cover and cook 1 minute. Serve with noodles. Serves 4 to 6.

*Note: For a more strongly flavored dish substitute 1 cup Oven Barbecued Pork (see recipe, page 75) for the pork shoulder. Stir-fry the barbecued pork for 2 minutes following the chicken, without adding more cooking oil.

Peppery Lamb with Green Onions

¾ **pound boneless lamb**
2 **tablespoons soy sauce**
1 **tablespoon dry sherry**
½ **teaspoon pepper**
2 **tablespoons cooking oil**
2 **cloves garlic, minced**
8 **green onions, bias-sliced into**
   1½-inch lengths

Partially freeze lamb; slice thinly into bite-size strips. In small bowl combine the soy sauce, dry sherry, and pepper. Set aside.

Preheat a wok or large skillet over high heat; add cooking oil. Stir-fry garlic in hot oil 30 seconds. Add meat; stir-fry 1½ minutes. Add green onions and soy mixture; stir-fry about 1½ minutes or till green onion is crisp-tender. Serve at once. Makes 3 or 4 servings.

Lamb with Kohlrabi

1 **pound boneless lamb**
2 **teaspoons cornstarch**
1 **tablespoon soy sauce**
3 **small kohlrabies**
½ **cup boiling water**
1 **teaspoon instant chicken**
   bouillon granules
2 **teaspoons cornstarch**
1 **teaspoon sugar**
1 **tablespoon soy sauce**
1 **tablespoon dry sherry**
2 **tablespoons cooking oil**
1 **clove garlic, minced**
1 **teaspoon grated gingerroot**
6 **green onions, bias-sliced into**
   1½-inch lengths
1 **tablespoon finely chopped**
   pickled ginger

Partially freeze lamb; slice thinly into bite-size strips. Sprinkle meat with 2 teaspoons cornstarch. Using your hands, work cornstarch into lamb. Add 1 tablespoon soy sauce; work into the meat. Let stand at room temperature 30 minutes.

Meanwhile, peel kohlrabies and cut into thin strips. In covered saucepan cook strips in a small amount of boiling salted water for 3 to 5 minutes. Drain well.

Combine boiling water with chicken bouillon, stirring till granules dissolve. Combine the remaining 2 teaspoons cornstarch and sugar; blend in remaining 1 tablespoon soy sauce and dry sherry. Stir soy mixture into chicken broth.

Preheat a wok or large skillet over high heat; add cooking oil. Stir-fry garlic and gingerroot in hot oil 30 seconds. Add kohlrabi; stir-fry 1 minute. Add green onions; stir-fry 1 minute more. Remove kohlrabi and green onions. (Add more oil, if necessary.) Add *half* the lamb to *hot* wok or skillet; stir-fry 2 to 3 minutes. Remove lamb. Stir-fry remaining lamb 2 to 3 minutes. Return all lamb to wok or skillet. Stir broth mixture; stir into lamb. Cook and stir till thickened. Stir in kohlrabi, green onions, and pickled ginger; cover and cook 2 minutes. Serve at once. Serves 4.

Garden Vegetable Stir-Fry

2 **medium carrots, cut in thirds**
2 **cups green beans bias-sliced**
   into 1-inch lengths
2 **cups sliced cauliflower**
2 **tablespoons cold water**
1½ **teaspoons cornstarch**
2 **tablespoons soy sauce**
1 **tablespoon dry sherry**
2 **teaspoons sugar**
   Dash pepper
2 **tablespoons cooking oil**
1 **medium onion, cut in thin**
   wedges
1 **cup sliced zucchini**

Cut carrots into thin sticks. In covered saucepan cook carrots and green beans in boiling salted water for 3 minutes. Add cauliflower. Cover and cook 2 minutes more; drain well. In small bowl blend water into cornstarch; stir in soy sauce, dry sherry, sugar, and pepper. Set aside.

Preheat a wok or large skillet over high heat; add cooking oil. Stir-fry onion in hot oil for 1 minute. Add carrots, green beans, cauliflower, and zucchini; stir-fry 2 minutes or till vegetables are crisp-tender. Stir soy mixture; stir into vegetables. Cook and stir 3 to 4 minutes or till thickened and bubbly. Serve at once. Serves 6.

Garden Vegetable Stir-Fry blends Oriental seasonings with American favorites such as carrots, beans, and cauliflower.

Asparagus-Tomato Stir-Fry

1 tablespoon water
1 teaspoon cornstarch
2 teaspoons soy sauce
¼ teaspoon salt
1 pound fresh asparagus
1 tablespoon cooking oil
4 green onions, bias-sliced into
    1-inch lengths
1½ cups sliced fresh mushrooms
2 small tomatoes, cut in thin
    wedges

Blend water into cornstarch; stir in soy sauce and salt. Set aside. Snap off and discard the woody bases from asparagus. Bias-slice asparagus crosswise into 1½-inch lengths. (If asparagus is not slender young stalks, precook for 4 to 5 minutes.)

Preheat a wok or large skillet over high heat; add cooking oil. Stir-fry asparagus and green onions in hot oil for 4 minutes. Add mushrooms; stir-fry 1 minute more. Stir soy mixture; stir into vegetables. Cook and stir till thickened and bubbly. Add tomatoes and heat through. Serve at once. Makes 6 servings.

Stir-Fried Pea Pods (pictured on page 2)

1½ teaspoons instant chicken
    bouillon granules
⅓ cup boiling water
1 tablespoon soy sauce
2 tablespoons cold water
2 teaspoons cornstarch
1 8-ounce can bamboo shoots
1 8-ounce can water chestnuts
1 6-ounce can whole mushrooms
2 tablespoons cooking oil
1 clove garlic, minced
2 6-ounce packages frozen pea
    pods, thawed

Dissolve bouillon granules in boiling water; stir in soy sauce. Blend cold water into cornstarch; stir into bouillon mixture. Set aside. Drain bamboo shoots, water chestnuts, and mushrooms; thinly slice water chestnuts.

Preheat a wok or large skillet over high heat; add cooking oil. Stir-fry garlic in hot oil for 30 seconds. Add bamboo shoots, water chestnuts, mushrooms, and pea pods; stir-fry 2 minutes. Stir chicken broth mixture; stir into vegetables. Cook and stir till thickened and bubbly. Cover and cook 1 minute more. Serve at once. Garnish with cashews, if desired. Makes 8 servings.

Sweet and Pungent Spinach

2 tablespoons water
2 tablespoons vinegar
1 tablespoon sugar
1 tablespoon cooking oil
¼ cup coarsely chopped peanuts
1 pound small fresh spinach leaves
    (12 cups)

Combine water, vinegar, and sugar. Set aside. Preheat a wok or large skillet over high heat; add cooking oil. Stir-fry peanuts in hot oil for 1 to 2 minutes or just till lightly toasted. Remove peanuts. Add spinach to wok; stir-fry 2 minutes or till crisp-tender. Stir vinegar mixture; stir into spinach. Add peanuts; heat through, tossing gently to mix. Serve at once. Makes 4 servings.

Skillet Cooking

Although the wok is the traditional utensil for Oriental cooking, you can enjoy the fun of preparing Oriental foods even if you don't own one. Any recipe that's cooked in a wok can also be prepared in a skillet. Just be sure to choose a large heavy skillet with deep sides, and keep the food moving constantly. This technique helps ensure that all the ingredients are cooked as quickly and evenly as possible.

Oriental Vegetable Toss

4 dried mushrooms
1 cup fresh pea pods *or* ½ of a
   6-ounce package frozen pea
   pods, thawed
½ teaspoon instant beef bouillon
   granules
¼ cup boiling water
2 teaspoons cornstarch
1 teaspoon sugar
½ teaspoon grated gingerroot
⅛ teaspoon freshly ground pepper
3 tablespoons soy sauce
2 tablespoons cooking oil
6 green onions, bias-sliced into
   1-inch lengths
2 cups chopped Chinese cabbage
1 cup fresh bean sprouts *or* ½ of a
   16-ounce can bean sprouts,
   drained
4 ounces fresh tofu (bean curd),
   cubed
1 medium tomato, cut into thin
   wedges

In small bowl soak mushrooms in enough warm water to cover for 30 minutes; squeeze to drain well. Chop mushrooms, discarding stems. Break off tips of fresh pea pods and remove strings. Halve pea pods lengthwise; set aside. Dissolve bouillon granules in boiling water. In small bowl stir together cornstarch, sugar, gingerroot, and pepper; blend in soy sauce. Stir in bouillon mixture; set aside.

Preheat a wok or large skillet over high heat; add cooking oil. Stir-fry green onions and pea pods in hot oil for 1 minute. Remove green onions and pea pods. Add Chinese cabbage and bean sprouts; stir-fry 1 minute. Add mushrooms; stir-fry 1 minute more. Stir soy mixture and stir into vegetables; cook and stir till thickened. Stir in green onions, pea pods, tofu, and tomato; cover and cook 1 minute. Serve at once. Serves 4.

Buddhist Vegetable Dish

1 ounce bean threads, broken into
   2-inch pieces (1½ cups)
   Boiling water
8 lily buds
4 dried mushrooms
   Warm water
½ medium head Chinese cabbage
1 medium zucchini
1 small green pepper
¾ cup cold water
4 teaspoons cornstarch
⅓ cup soy sauce
3 tablespoons dry sherry
2 tablespoons cooking oil
½ cup raw peanuts
1 stalk celery, cut into 1-inch slices
   (½ cup)
½ cup chopped onion
2 cups fresh bean sprouts *or* 1
   16-ounce can bean sprouts,
   drained

In a large bowl soak bean threads in enough boiling water to cover for 30 minutes. Drain well; squeeze out excess moisture. In separate small bowls soak lily buds and dried mushrooms in enough warm water to cover for 30 minutes. Drain. Cut lily buds into 1-inch lengths, discarding tough stem ends. Squeeze mushrooms to drain well. Cut mushrooms into thin strips, discarding stems. Chop Chinese cabbage. Cut zucchini crosswise into 4 equal pieces. Halve each piece lengthwise; cut into strips. Cut green pepper into 2x⅛-inch strips. Blend cold water into cornstarch; stir in soy sauce and sherry. Set aside.

Preheat a wok or large skillet over high heat; add the cooking oil. Stir-fry peanuts in hot oil 2 to 3 minutes or till lightly browned. Remove peanuts. (Add more oil, if necessary.) Add celery and onion; stir-fry 2 minutes. Remove celery and onion. Add zucchini and green pepper; stir-fry 2 minutes. Remove zucchini and green pepper. Add Chinese cabbage; stir-fry 2 minutes. Remove Chinese cabbage. Add bean threads, lily buds, mushrooms, and bean sprouts; stir-fry 1 minute. Stir soy mixture and stir into vegetables. Cook and stir till thickened. Stir in peanuts, celery, onion, zucchini, green pepper, and Chinese cabbage; cover and cook 2 minutes more. Serve at once. Serves 6 to 8.

Wontons, Tempura, and Other Fried Favorites

Beef-and Shrimp-Filled Wontons

- 1 beaten egg
- 1 cup finely chopped bok choy or cabbage
- ¼ cup finely chopped green onion or leeks
- 2 tablespoons soy sauce
- 1 tablespoon grated gingerroot
- ¼ teaspoon sugar
- ⅛ teaspoon salt
- ½ pound ground beef or ground pork
- 1 4½-ounce can shrimp, drained and chopped
- 40 wonton skins
  Cooking oil for deep-fat frying
  Sauces (see recipes, pages 84 and 85)

Wrapping wontons: fill wonton, then fold and tuck point under filling as shown. Roll wonton once.

For filling, in large mixing bowl combine egg, bok choy or cabbage, green onion or leeks, soy sauce, gingerroot, sugar, salt, and dash *pepper*. Add ground beef or pork, and chopped shrimp; mix well.

Position wonton skin with one point toward you. Spoon 2 teaspoonfuls of filling just off center of skin. Fold bottom point of wonton skin over the filling; tuck point under filling as shown. Roll once to cover filling, leaving about 1 inch unrolled at the top of the skin. Moisten the right-hand corner of skin with water. Grasp the right- and left-hand corners of skin as shown; bring these corners toward you below the filling. Overlap the left-hand corner over the right-hand corner; press the wonton skin securely to seal.

Fry wontons, a few at a time, in deep hot oil (365°) for 2 to 3 minutes or till golden (refer to tip box on page 27). Drain on paper toweling. Serve warm with one or two sauces (see recipes on pages 84 and 85). Makes about 40 wontons.

Substitution tips: When you're ready to fix wontons and the skins are not available, purchase egg roll skins instead. Ten egg roll skins cut into quarters will give you forty skins the same size as wonton skins.

Interchange the tasty fillings on pages 25 and 26 to make either wontons or egg rolls for your family and guests.

Grasp wonton corners and bring together below filling as arrows indicate. Overlap corners and press to seal.

Wrapping egg rolls (see recipe, page 26): Fold and roll skin over filling as for wontons. Then fold sides in.

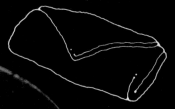

Moisten edges of skin and then roll up egg roll into a neat bundle. Press to seal.

Chicken and Vegetable Egg Rolls

½ cup dried mushrooms
1 whole large chicken breast,
   skinned, split, and boned
1 clove garlic, minced
1 tablespoon cooking oil
1 16-ounce can bean sprouts,
   drained
2 cups small spinach leaves
½ cup thinly sliced green onion
½ cup thinly sliced bamboo shoots
2 tablespoons soy sauce
2 teaspoons cornstarch
1 teaspoon grated gingerroot
½ teaspoon sugar
¼ teaspoon salt
12 egg roll skins
   Cooking oil for deep-fat frying

Soak mushrooms in warm water for 30 minutes; drain and chop, discarding stems. Chop chicken. For filling, stir-fry chicken and garlic quickly in 1 tablespoon hot oil about 2 minutes. Add vegetables; stir-fry about 3 minutes more. Blend soy into cornstarch; stir in gingerroot, sugar, and salt. Stir into chicken mixture; cook and stir till thickened. Cool.

Place egg roll skin with one point toward you (see sketches on page 25). Spoon ¼ cup of filling diagonally across and just below center of skin. Fold bottom point of skin over filling; tuck point under filling. Fold side corners over, forming envelope shape as shown. Roll up toward remaining corner; moisten point and press firmly to seal. Repeat with remaining egg roll skins and filling.

Fry egg rolls, a few at a time, in deep hot oil (365°) for 2 to 3 minutes or till golden brown (refer to tip box on page 27). Drain on paper toweling. Serve warm with one or two sauces (see recipes on pages 84 and 85). Makes 12 egg rolls.

Chicken and Crab Filling

1 whole small chicken breast
1 clove garlic, minced
1 tablespoon cooking oil
1 cup chopped Chinese cabbage
½ cup finely chopped pea pods
¼ cup chopped water chestnuts
2 tablespoons chopped onion
½ cup canned *or* cooked crab meat
1 beaten egg
2 tablespoons soy sauce
1 teaspoon dry sherry
40 wonton skins *or* 6 egg roll skins
   Cooking oil for deep-fat frying

Skin, split, and bone chicken; finely chop. In skillet stir-fry chicken and garlic in the 1 tablespoon hot cooking oil about 2 minutes. Add vegetables; stir-fry 2 to 3 minutes more. Flake crab meat. In bowl combine crab, chicken-vegetable mixture, egg, soy sauce, sherry, ¼ teaspoon *salt,* and ⅛ teaspoon *pepper.* Cool slightly.

Wrap wontons using directions on page 25, or follow directions above for wrapping egg rolls. Fry wontons or egg rolls, a few at a time, in deep hot oil (365°) for 2 to 3 minutes or till golden brown. Using a slotted spoon or wire strainer remove wontons or egg rolls. Drain on paper toweling. Serve warm with one or two sauces (see recipes on pages 84 and 85). Makes 40 wontons or 6 egg rolls.

Pork and Shrimp Filling

½ pound ground pork
1 clove garlic, minced
1 tablespoon cooking oil
2 cups finely chopped bok choy
1 cup chopped fresh mushrooms
½ cup finely chopped onion
½ cup finely chopped celery
½ cup chopped water chestnuts
¼ cup shredded carrot
1 4½-ounce can shrimp
1 beaten egg
2 tablespoons soy sauce
1 tablespoon dry sherry
½ teaspoon sugar
40 wonton skins *or* 6 egg roll skins
   Cooking oil for deep-fat frying

In skillet stir-fry pork and garlic quickly in 1 tablespoon hot oil till meat is browned. Drain off fat. Add vegetables; stir-fry 2 to 3 minutes more. Drain shrimp and chop. In bowl combine shrimp, pork-vegetable mixture, egg, soy sauce, sherry, sugar, and ¼ teaspoon *salt.* Cool slightly.

Wrap wontons using directions on page 25, or follow directions above for wrapping egg rolls. Fry wontons or egg rolls, a few at a time, in deep hot oil (365°) for 2 to 3 minutes or till golden brown. Using a slotted spoon or wire strainer remove wontons or egg rolls. Drain on paper toweling. Serve warm with one or two sauces (see recipes on pages 84 and 85). Makes 40 wontons or 6 egg rolls.

Tempura *Japanese*

1 pound fresh *or* frozen large
   shrimp
1 12-ounce package frozen halibut
   steaks
1 cup all-purpose flour
2 tablespoons cornstarch
1 cup ice water
1 egg yolk
2 stiffly beaten egg whites
   Peanut oil *or* cooking oil for
   deep-fat frying
½ pound fresh green beans, cut
   into 2-inch lengths
½ pound fresh asparagus spears,
   cut into 2-inch lengths
2 medium sweet potatoes, peeled
   and sliced ¼ inch thick
1 small eggplant, peeled and cut
   into 1-inch cubes
1 cup fresh mushrooms, halved
   Parsley sprigs
   Tempura Sauce
   Tempura Condiments

Thaw shrimp, if frozen. Shell and devein shrimp. Thaw frozen halibut; cut halibut into 1-inch pieces. To make batter, stir together flour, cornstarch, and ½ teaspoon *salt*. Make a well in center of dry ingredients. Combine ice water and egg yolk; add all at once to dry ingredients. Slowly stir just till moistened (do not overbeat; a few lumps should remain). Fold in egg whites. Do not allow batter to stand more than a few minutes before using.

Pour peanut or cooking oil into an electric fondue cooker to depth of 2 inches. Heat oil on range to 425°. Add 1 teaspoon *salt*. Turn fondue burner to highest setting. Transfer cooker to fondue burner. (*Or,* fry Tempura in deep hot fat (400°) in deep fat fryer or heavy saucepan.)

Dip shrimp, halibut, and vegetable pieces into batter, swirling to coat. Fry, a few pieces at a time, in hot oil 2 to 3 minutes. Drain. Pass Tempura Sauce and Tempura Condiments. Makes 6 to 8 servings.

Tempura Sauce: In saucepan mix 1 cup *water*, ¼ cup *dry sherry*, ¼ cup *soy sauce*, 1 teaspoon *sugar,* and 1 teaspoon instant *chicken bouillon granules*. Cook and stir till boiling.

Tempura Condiments: (1) grated *gingerroot;* (2) equal parts grated *turnip* and *radish,* mixed; (3) ½ cup prepared *mustard* mixed with 3 tablespoons *soy sauce.*

Deep-Fat Frying Pointers

It's easy to deep-fry foods perfectly so they're crisp on the outside and tender and moist on the inside. Just use the following hints.

First, it's important to select the right type of equipment for successful deep-fat frying. The wok works very well because it has a large cooking surface. If you don't own a wok, substitute a heavy skillet or pan that's at least 3 inches deep. This allows for 1½ to 2 inches of cooking oil. (You'll need about 3 to 4 cups oil for a wok, or about 10 cups oil for a deep 12-inch skillet.) An electric deep-fat fryer is also excellent to use.

For deep-fat frying use oil that can be heated to a high temperature without smoking. Your best choices are cottonseed, corn, or peanut oil.

Take the guesswork out of frying by using a deep-fat thermometer to assure that the oil reaches and maintains the desired temperature. For an accurate reading, the thermometer must not touch the bottom of the pan.

Food should be added gradually to the hot oil—a few pieces at a time, rather than all at once. For maximum crispness, remember to return oil to the proper temperature before frying more food.

After you're done frying, take care of the oil so it can be reused. Allow oil to cool, strain through a double thickness of cheesecloth, then store in a covered jar. When you reuse the oil, add equal amounts of fresh oil to help avoid smoking and possible flare-ups.

Soft-Fried Eggs and Pork in Mandarin Pancakes

Mandarin Pancakes
¼ **cup dried lily buds**
¼ **cup dried tree ears**
1 **cup hot water**
½ **pound boneless pork *or* beef top round, cut ½ inch thick**
1 **tablespoon cooking oil**
¼ **cup thinly sliced bamboo shoots**
2 **tablespoons soy sauce**
1 **teaspoon sugar**
1 **teaspoon grated gingerroot**
½ **teaspoon salt**
¼ **teaspoon pepper**
5 **beaten eggs**

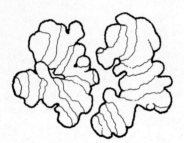

Prepare the Mandarin Pancakes; set aside.

In small bowl combine lily buds and tree ears; pour in hot water. Let soak for 30 minutes. Rinse and squeeze to drain thoroughly. Cut lily buds into 1-inch pieces. Thinly slice the tree ears.

Partially freeze the pork or beef. Cut partially frozen meat into 1x¼-inch strips. In skillet cook meat in hot oil about 4 minutes or till lightly browned. Stir in lily buds, tree ears, the bamboo shoots, soy sauce, sugar, gingerroot, salt, and pepper. Cook and stir till heated through. Add beaten eggs to mixture. Turn heat to low. Cook eggs about 5 minutes or till cooked but still glossy and moist. (Don't stir eggs till mixture starts to set on bottom. Avoid breaking up eggs any more than necessary.) Remove meat and egg mixture from the heat.

Meanwhile, layer Mandarin Pancakes between pieces of foil on a foil-lined baking sheet; cover and heat in 375° oven about 7 minutes or till heated through. (Or, to micro-cook, use a 12x7x2-inch nonmetal baking dish and place pancakes between layers of waxed paper. Cover with waxed paper; cook in countertop microwave oven for 1½ to 2 minutes.)

Spoon about ¼ cup of the hot meat and egg mixture in center of unbrowned side of each Mandarin Pancake. Fold two opposite edges of pancake so they overlap about 1 inch atop mixture. Starting at unfolded edge roll pancake as for jelly roll, making sure folded sides are included in roll. Keep warm while rolling remaining pancakes. Serve immediately. (Pancakes are eaten with the fingers.) Makes 5 or 6 servings.

Mandarin Pancakes: Stir together 1½ cups all-purpose *flour* and ¼ teaspoon *salt.* Pour ½ cup *boiling water* slowly into flour, stirring constantly with a fork or chopsticks. Stir till well blended. Stir in 3 tablespoons cold *water.* When cool enough to handle, knead in 2 tablespoons all-purpose *flour* till smooth and elastic (8 to 10 minutes). Shape dough into a ball. Place the dough back in bowl; cover with damp towel. Let stand for 15 to 20 minutes.

Turn dough out on lightly floured surface. Form into a 12-inch-long roll. Cut roll into 1-inch pieces. Flatten each piece of dough with the palm of the hand. To make pancakes, roll each piece of dough into a 6-inch circle. Brush the entire surface of one side of each pancake lightly with *shortening, cooking oil,* or *sesame oil.*

Stack two pancakes together, greased sides together. (These delicate pancakes are always cooked in pairs because, when rolled out, they are too fragile to cook individually.) In a heavy ungreased skillet or griddle cook the pancake stacks, a few at a time, over medium heat 20 to 30 seconds on each side or till bubbles appear on surface of pancake (a few golden spots will appear). Quickly remove from pan and gently separate the paired pancakes. Place all the pancakes on baking sheet or in a baking dish; cover with a dry towel or plastic wrap to keep moist. Repeat with remaining pancakes. Makes 12 pancakes.

Mandarin-Style Pot Stickers

2 cups finely chopped Chinese
    cabbage *or* bok choy
½ pound ground pork *or* ground
    beef
1 4½-ounce can shrimp, drained
    and chopped
1 4-ounce can chopped
    mushrooms, drained
2 tablespoons finely chopped
    onion
2 tablespoons soy sauce
2 teaspoons sesame oil
1 teaspoon salt
1 teaspoon grated gingerroot
3 cups all-purpose flour
½ teaspoon salt
1 cup boiling water
⅓ cup cold water
¼ cup all-purpose flour
3 tablespoons soy sauce
3 tablespoons rice vinegar *or* white
    vinegar
    Cooking oil
    Water

Place the Chinese cabbage or bok choy in a double layer of cheesecloth or paper toweling; press tightly to extract as much moisture as possible.

Combine cabbage or bok choy, pork or beef, shrimp, mushrooms, onion, the 2 tablespoons soy sauce, sesame oil, the 1 teaspoon salt, and gingerroot. Cover and refrigerate.

To prepare the dumplings, stir together the 3 cups flour and the ½ teaspoon salt. Pour the boiling water slowly into flour, stirring constantly. Stir till well blended. Stir in the ⅓ cup cold water. When cool enough to handle, knead dough on a well floured surface, kneading in the ¼ cup flour till dough is smooth and elastic (8 to 10 minutes). Shape dough into a ball. Place dough back in bowl; cover with a damp towel. Let stand for 15 to 20 minutes.

Meanwhile, combine the 3 tablespoons soy sauce and vinegar for dipping sauce; set aside. Turn dough out on lightly floured surface. Divide dough into four equal portions. Roll each portion to ⅛-inch thickness. Cut into 3-inch rounds with cookie cutter. Cut into at least 40 rounds (reroll as needed). Spoon about 1 tablespoon of filling in center of one of the rounds. Fold round in half across filling and pinch edges to seal. Set pinched edge of dumpling upright and press gently to slightly flatten the bottom. Transfer dumpling to a floured cookie sheet. Cover with dry towel. Repeat with the remaining filling and rounds.

In 12-inch skillet heat *2 tablespoons* oil about 1 minute or till very hot. Set *half* of the dumplings upright in skillet (making sure dumplings do not touch each other); cook in hot oil about 1 minute or till bottoms are lightly browned. Add ⅔ *cup* water to skillet. Cover; cook about 10 minutes. Uncover and cook 2 to 3 minutes or till all water evaporates. Add *1 table-spoon* oil to skillet; gently swirl oil about skillet. Cook dumplings, uncovered, for 1 minute more. Using a wide spatula gently remove dumplings from skillet. Keep warm while cooking remaining dumplings. Serve with dipping sauce. Makes 40 appetizers.

Sweet-Sour Pork

1 pound boneless pork
1 beaten egg
¼ cup cornstarch
¼ cup all-purpose flour
1¼ cups Homemade Chicken Broth
    (see recipe, page 54)
    Cooking oil for deep-fat frying
1 large green pepper, diced
½ cup chopped carrot
1 clove garlic, minced
2 tablespoons cooking oil
½ cup sugar
⅓ cup red wine vinegar
2 teaspoons soy sauce
2 tablespoons cornstarch

Trim excess fat from pork; cut pork into 1-inch cubes. In a bowl combine egg, the ¼ cup cornstarch, flour, ¼ *cup* of the chicken broth, and ½ teaspoon *salt*; beat till smooth. Dip pork cubes in batter. Fry in deep hot oil (365°) for 5 to 6 minutes or till golden. Drain; keep warm. In skillet cook green pepper, carrot, and garlic in the 2 tablespoons oil till vegetables are tender but not brown. Stir in remaining 1 cup chicken broth, sugar, vinegar, and soy sauce. Bring to boiling; boil rapidly 1 minute. Slowly blend ¼ cup cold *water* into the 2 tablespoons cornstarch. Stir into vegetable mixture. Cook and stir till thickened and bubbly. Stir in pork cubes. Serve with hot cooked rice, if desired. Makes 4 to 6 servings.

Szechwan Fried Pork Chops

4 **pork rib chops, cut ½ inch thick
    (1½ pounds)**
¼ **cup thinly sliced green onion**
¼ **cup soy sauce**
1 **tablespoon grated gingerroot**
1 **teaspoon sugar**
1 **teaspoon sesame oil *or* cooking
    oil**
½ **cup cornstarch**
1 **cup cooking oil**

Remove the bone and trim excess fat from each pork chop. Score each piece diagonally, making diamond-shaped cuts. Pound pork pieces to about a ⅛-inch thickness. Place pork in a shallow baking dish.

   For the marinade, combine onion, soy sauce, gingerroot, sugar, and the 1 teaspoon sesame oil or cooking oil. Pour marinade mixture over pork. Marinate at room temperature for 20 minutes, turning twice; drain. Dip chops in cornstarch, making sure both sides are thoroughly coated. In a 12-inch skillet fry chops in 1 cup hot oil about 1 minute on each side. Drain on paper toweling. Serves 4.

Breaded Pork Cutlets *Japanese*

1 **pound pork tenderloin, cut
    crosswise into 6 pieces**
¼ **cup dry sherry**
¼ **cup soy sauce**
1 **clove garlic, minced**
½ **cup all-purpose flour**
1 **beaten egg**
2 **tablespoons thinly sliced green
    onion**
¾ **cup fine dry bread crumbs**
3 **tablespoons cooking oil
    Pickled ginger, cut into thin
    slices, *or* lemon slices**

Pound pork to ¼- to ⅛-inch thickness. Cut small slits around edges to prevent curling. Place pork in shallow baking dish. To prepare marinade, stir together dry sherry, soy sauce, and garlic. Pour marinade over pork. Marinate at room temperature for 30 minutes, turning pork twice; drain. Combine flour, ¼ teaspoon *salt*, and ⅛ teaspoon *pepper*. Combine egg, onion, and 1 tablespoon *water*. Coat meat with flour mixture; dip cutlets in egg mixture, then in bread crumbs.

   In large skillet cook *half* the cutlets in hot oil 2 to 3 minutes on each side. Remove from pan to platter; keep warm. Add a little more oil, if necessary. Repeat with the remaining cutlets. If desired, thinly slice cutlets crosswise to serve. Garnish with pickled ginger or lemon. Makes 6 servings.

Sweet and Pungent Spareribs

3 **pounds meaty pork spareribs,
    sawed in half across bones**
¼ **cup dry sherry**
¼ **cup soy sauce**
1 **tablespoon Homemade Five
    Spice Powder**
1 **tablespoon vinegar**
½ **teaspoon salt**
⅛ **teaspoon pepper**
1 **beaten egg**
¼ **cup cornstarch**
¼ **cup all-purpose flour
    Cooking oil for deep-fat frying
    Lettuce leaves
    Sweet and Pungent Sauce (see
    recipe, page 84)**

Cut meat in 2-rib portions. Simmer, covered, in boiling water for 30 minutes; drain. Place ribs in shallow baking dish.

   To prepare marinade, combine dry sherry, soy sauce, five spice powder, vinegar, salt, and pepper. Pour marinade over ribs. Marinate at room temperature about 30 minutes, turning ribs once. Drain; reserve marinade. To make batter, combine reserved marinade, egg, cornstarch, and flour; beat till smooth. Dip ribs in batter. Fry spareribs, a few at a time, in deep hot oil (365°) for 1 to 2 minutes or till golden brown. Drain on paper toweling. Keep warm while cooking remaining ribs. Place ribs atop lettuce on platter; spoon some Sweet and Pungent Sauce over. Pass remaining sauce. Serves 4 or 5.

   Homemade Five Spice Powder: In small bowl combine 1 teaspoon ground *cinnamon;* 1 teaspoon crushed *aniseed* or 1 *star anise,* ground; ¼ teaspoon crushed *fennel seed;* ¼ teaspoon freshly ground *pepper* or ¼ teaspoon crushed *Szechwan pepper;* and ⅛ teaspoon ground *cloves.* Store in covered container. (Or, purchase commercial five spice powder at Oriental stores.)

For an intriguing, delightfully tempting main dish, make *Sweet and Pungent Spareribs* for your next Chinese dinner.

Pork and Shrimp Egg Foo Yung

½ **pound boneless pork**
1 **clove garlic, minced**
1 **tablespoon cooking oil**
1 **cup finely chopped Chinese**
   cabbage
½ **cup chopped green pepper**
½ **cup chopped onion**
1 **tablespoon Homemade Oyster**
   Sauce (see recipe, page 85) *or*
   ½ **teaspoon salt**
1 **teaspoon instant beef bouillon**
   granules
1 **teaspoon molasses**
1 **teaspoon soy sauce**
¼ **teaspoon sugar**
2 **tablespoons cold water**
1 **tablespoon cornstarch**
6 **eggs**
1 **4½-ounce can shrimp, drained**
   and chopped
   Cooking oil for frying

Using cleaver or knife, chop pork. In skillet or wok stir-fry pork and garlic in the 1 tablespoon hot oil till meat is browned. Drain off fat. Add Chinese cabbage, green pepper, and onion; cook and stir 2 to 3 minutes more. Cool.

To prepare sauce, in saucepan combine the oyster sauce or ½ teaspoon salt, beef bouillon granules, molasses, soy sauce, sugar, and 1 cup *water.* Bring to boiling. Blend 2 tablespoons cold water into cornstarch; stir into hot mixture. Cook and stir till thickened and bubbly. Turn to low heat; keep warm while frying egg foo yung mixture.

To make egg foo yung, beat together eggs, 1 teaspoon *salt,* and ¼ teaspoon *pepper.* Stir in the cooled pork-vegetable mixture. Stir in shrimp; mix well. In skillet heat about 2 tablespoons oil till hot. Using about ¼ cup of the mixture for each patty, fry patties in hot oil about 1 minute per side or till golden. (Spread the meat mixture to cover egg as the egg spreads slightly.) Keep warm. Repeat till all the mixture is used, stirring each time; add more oil as needed. Serve sauce with egg foo yung. Makes 5 or 6 servings.

Japanese-Style Skewered Chicken

3 **whole small chicken breasts,**
   skinned, split, and boned
6 **green onions**
¾ **cup all-purpose flour**
½ **teaspoon salt**
½ **cup ice water**
1 **beaten egg**
   Cooking oil for deep-fat frying
2 **tablespoons dijon-style mustard**
   or **prepared mustard**
1 **tablespoon soy sauce**

Cut chicken into 1¼x1¼-inch pieces. Cut each green onion into 1-inch-long pieces. On twelve short bamboo skewers alternate pieces of chicken and green onion.

To prepare batter, in a pie plate or shallow dish stir together flour and salt. Combine ice water and egg; mix well. Add egg mixture all at once to the flour; stir just till moistened. Dip skewers into batter, swirling to coat evenly. Carefully place four skewers in deep hot oil (365°). Fry about 5 minutes or till chicken is lightly browned. Turn skewers once during frying. Drain on paper toweling. Keep warm while cooking the remaining skewers. Blend together mustard and soy sauce; serve with chicken as a dipping sauce. Serves 12.

Soy-Marinated Fried Chicken Nuggets *Japanese*

4 **whole large chicken breasts,**
   skinned, split, and boned
¼ **cup soy sauce**
¼ **cup dry sherry, sake,** *or* **mirin**
1 **tablespoon grated gingerroot**
2 **cloves garlic, minced**
1 **teaspoon sugar**
   Cornstarch
   Cooking oil for deep-fat frying
2 **green onions**
   Plum Sauce (see recipe, page 85)

Cut chicken into 1-inch pieces. To prepare marinade, in bowl combine soy sauce; dry sherry, sake, or mirin; gingerroot; garlic; and sugar. Add chicken. Marinate about 30 minutes at room temperature; stir once or twice. Drain.

Roll the chicken pieces in cornstarch to coat evenly (use about ½ cup); shake to remove excess cornstarch. Fry chicken pieces, several at a time, in deep hot oil (365°) for 2 to 3 minutes or till golden. Using slotted spoon or wire strainer, remove pieces and drain on paper toweling. Keep warm while cooking the remaining chicken. Arrange on heated serving platter. Cut green onions in 1-inch lengths; cut pieces into thin lengthwise strips. Sprinkle atop chicken. Serve with Plum Sauce. Makes 8 servings.

Deep-Fried Curried Chicken

4 large chicken thighs, skinned
    and boned or 2 whole large
    chicken breasts, skinned, split,
    and boned
½ cup all-purpose flour
1 teaspoon salt
⅛ teaspoon ground ginger
⅛ teaspoon pepper
2 slightly beaten eggs
2 tablespoons water
    Cooking oil for deep-fat frying
¾ cup Homemade Chicken Broth
    (see recipe, page 54)
3 tablespoons dry sherry
2 tablespoons finely chopped
    onion
2 tablespoons finely snipped
    parsley
1½ teaspoons curry powder
½ teaspoon sugar
2 tablespoons cold water
2 teaspoons cornstarch
½ head lettuce, shredded

Cut chicken into 1-inch pieces. In a bowl combine flour, salt, ginger, and pepper; mix well. Stir together eggs and 2 tablespoons water. Stir egg mixture into dry ingredients all at once; mix well. Dip chicken in flour mixture, swirling to coat thoroughly. Fry chicken pieces, several at a time, in deep hot oil (365°) for 2 to 3 minutes or till golden. Using a slotted spoon or wire strainer, remove pieces and drain on paper toweling. Keep warm while cooking the remaining chicken.

In a small saucepan stir together the chicken broth, dry sherry, onion, parsley, curry, and sugar; bring to boiling. Slowly blend 2 tablespoons cold water into cornstarch. Stir into hot mixture. Cook and stir till thickened and bubbly. Arrange the shredded lettuce on individual plates; top with fried chicken pieces. Pour the curry sauce over all and serve. Makes 4 to 6 servings.

Fried Chicken with Crab Sauce

2 whole large chicken breasts,
    skinned, split, and boned
1 tablespoon sugar
1 tablespoon cornstarch or
    all-purpose flour
1 teaspoon salt
¾ teaspoon Homemade Five Spice
    Powder (see recipe, page 31)
⅛ teaspoon dry mustard
1 3-ounce can sliced mushrooms,
    drained
4 green onions, bias-sliced into
    1½-inch lengths
1 teaspoon grated gingerroot
1 tablespoon cooking oil
1 cup Homemade Chicken Broth
    (see recipe, page 54)
¼ teaspoon salt
⅛ teaspoon pepper
1 7½-ounce can crab meat,
    drained, flaked, and cartilage
    removed
1 tablespoon cold water
1 tablespoon cornstarch
    Cooking oil for deep-fat frying

Thoroughly rub the chicken breasts with mixture of sugar, 1 tablespoon cornstarch or flour, the 1 teaspoon salt, five spice powder, and dry mustard. Cover chicken and let stand at room temperature for 30 to 40 minutes. Cut chicken into 1½-inch pieces.

Meanwhile, prepare the crab sauce. In small saucepan stir-fry mushrooms, green onions, and gingerroot in the 1 tablespoon hot oil for about 1 minute. Stir in chicken broth, the ¼ teaspoon salt, and pepper. Bring to boiling, stirring occasionally. Stir in crab. Slowly blend cold water into 1 tablespoon cornstarch. Stir into saucepan mixture. Cook and stir till thickened and bubbly. Keep warm while frying chicken.

Fry chicken pieces, half at a time, in deep hot oil (365°) about 2 minutes or till golden brown. Using a slotted spoon or wire strainer, remove and drain on paper toweling.

To serve, arrange chicken pieces on serving platter and pour the crab sauce over. Makes 6 to 8 servings.

Japanese Omelet

½ cup finely shredded Chinese
    white radish *or* radish
4 ounces fresh tofu (bean curd)
6 beaten eggs
2 teaspoons soy sauce
1 teaspoon sugar
1 teaspoon mirin *or* dry sherry
½ teaspoon salt
½ cup finely chopped cooked
    chicken, shrimp, *or* ham
½ cup finely chopped fresh
    mushrooms *or* 1 3-ounce can
    chopped mushrooms, drained
½ cup cooked peas
2 tablespoons thinly sliced green
    onion
1 teaspoon cooking oil

Place radish in double thickness of cheesecloth or paper toweling and press tightly to extract as much moisture as possible; set aside. Place tofu in double thickness of cheesecloth or paper toweling; press tightly as above. Mash tofu with a fork; set aside. In bowl combine eggs, soy sauce, sugar, mirin or dry sherry, and salt. Stir in chicken, shrimp, or ham; mushrooms; peas; green onion; and mashed tofu.

Heat an 8x6-inch *tamago-yaki nabe* (Japanese rectangular omelet pan) or a 10-inch skillet; add cooking oil. Lift and rotate pan so oil covers bottom of pan in a thin, even layer. Pour egg mixture into pan. Cook, covered, over medium-low heat for 12 to 14 minutes or till mixture is just set in center and lightly browned on sides. Carefully loosen omelet and invert onto serving plate. Cut into 2x1½-inch pieces. Garnish each serving with a small amount of the shredded radish. Pass additional soy sauce, if desired. Makes 4 to 6 servings.

Paper-Wrapped Bundles

1 whole large chicken breast,
    skinned, split, and boned
1 tablespoon thinly sliced green
    onion
1 tablespoon dry sherry
1 tablespoon soy sauce
1 teaspoon sugar
1 teaspoon grated gingerroot
½ teaspoon salt
½ teaspoon dry mustard
    Few drops bottled hot pepper
    sauce
    Parchment paper, cut in 5-inch
    squares (about 32 squares)
½ of a 6-ounce package frozen pea
    pods, thawed and halved
    lengthwise *or* 1 cup fresh pea
    pods, halved lengthwise
6 green onions, bias-sliced into
    1½-inch lengths
½ cup sliced bamboo shoots
    Cooking oil for deep-fat frying

Partially freeze chicken. Thinly slice into bite-size strips.

For marinade, in a small deep bowl combine the 1 tablespoon green onion, dry sherry, soy sauce, sugar, gingerroot, salt, dry mustard, and hot pepper sauce; mix well. Add chicken to marinade. Marinate at room temperature about 30 minutes, turning chicken twice; drain.

Position one parchment square with one point toward you. To fill, place a few pieces of pea pods, 1 piece of green onion, 1 piece of bamboo shoot, and 1 piece of chicken horizontally across and just below center of parchment square. Fold bottom point of parchment over filling. Crease paper to hold the fold; tuck point under filling. Fold in side corners, overlapping slightly, forming envelope shape. Crease paper to hold the fold. Fold the remaining corner down so the tip extends beyond the bottom of bundle. Tuck the tip underneath the folded corners. Crease paper to hold the fold. Repeat with the remaining squares and filling.

Fry the parchment bundles, a few at a time, in deep hot oil (365°) for 1 to 1½ minutes. Drain on paper toweling. *Serve immediately.* To eat, unwrap the parchment using a fork or chopsticks. Makes about 32 bundles.

Variations for the filling: Use ½ pound fresh or frozen *shrimp,* shelled, deveined, and cut in half lengthwise; *or* ½ pound fresh or frozen *fish fillets,* cut into 1½x¼-inch pieces; *or* ½ pound boneless *beef sirloin,* partially frozen and cut into 2x¼-inch pieces. Add shrimp, fish, or beef to marinade in place of chicken.

Paper-Wrapped Bundles is a unique Chinese recipe for deep-frying pieces of chicken, beef, fish, and shrimp.

Soy-Sauced Salmon Steaks *Japanese*

4 **fresh *or* frozen salmon steaks *or* other fish steaks**
   Salt
2 **tablespoons cooking oil**
8 **slices of lemon**
2 **tablespoons soy sauce**
1 **tablespoon mirin *or* dry sherry**
   Pickled ginger *or* 1 medium cucumber, cut in strips

Thaw fish, if frozen. Sprinkle fish steaks with salt; let stand for 10 minutes. In large skillet cook fish in hot oil about 5 minutes or till browned on one side. Turn fish and add one slice of the lemon atop each steak; cook fish about 5 minutes more or till browned on other side. Discard cooked lemon slices. Combine soy sauce and mirin or dry sherry; pour over fish steaks. Cook over low heat for 1 to 2 minutes, turning steaks frequently. Remove fish to platter. Pour pan juices over steaks, top with remaining lemon slices. Garnish with pickled ginger or cucumber. Makes 4 servings.

Shrimp-Stuffed Mushrooms *Japanese*

½ **cup finely shredded Chinese white radish *or* radish**
24 **fresh medium mushrooms**
¼ **cup chopped green onion**
1 **tablespoon cooking oil**
2 **teaspoons all-purpose flour**
   Dash pepper
1 **4½-ounce can shrimp, drained and finely chopped**
⅓ **cup Homemade Chicken Broth (see recipe, page 54)**
3 **tablespoons soy sauce**
2 **tablespoons mirin *or* dry sherry**
½ **cup all-purpose flour**
1 **tablespoon cornstarch**
½ **cup ice water**
   Cooking oil for deep-fat frying

Place radish in a double layer of paper toweling; press tightly to extract as much moisture as possible. Set aside.

Remove mushroom stems; reserve caps. Chop stems. Cook stems and green onion in the 1 tablespoon of hot oil just till tender. Blend in the 2 teaspoons flour and pepper. Cook and stir till thickened; stir in shrimp. Stuff caps with mixture.

To prepare the dipping sauce, in saucepan combine chicken broth, soy sauce, and mirin or dry sherry; bring to boil. Remove from heat and pour into small bowl. Set aside.

For batter, stir together the ½ cup flour and cornstarch. Add ice water all at once to flour mixture; stir just till moistened. Dip mushrooms into batter, swirling to coat evenly. Fry mushrooms, a few at a time, in the deep hot oil (365°) about 4 minutes or till lightly golden brown, turning mushrooms occasionally. Remove mushrooms; drain on paper toweling. Keep warm while cooking remaining mushrooms.

To serve, arrange mushrooms on a serving platter with radish mounded in the center. Dip mushrooms into sauce and eat with the shredded radish. Makes 24 appetizers.

Somen-Coated Shrimp *Japanese*

1 **pound fresh *or* frozen *large* shrimp**
   Salt
1 **tablespoon cornstarch**
2 **slightly beaten egg whites**
3 **ounces somen (thin white noodles), broken into ½-inch lengths**
   Cooking oil for deep-fat frying
   Mirin-Soy Dipping Sauce

Thaw shrimp, if frozen; shell and devein shrimp. Press shrimp between layers of paper toweling to thoroughly dry. Lightly sprinkle shrimp with salt. Toss shrimp with cornstarch in a plastic bag, half at a time. Dip each shrimp in egg white; roll in noodles, pressing to coat well.

Fry shrimp, a few at a time, in deep hot oil (365°) for 2 to 3 minutes or till noodles turn golden; turn occasionally. Remove shrimp with slotted spoon or wire strainer; drain on paper toweling. Keep warm while cooking remaining shrimp. Serve with Mirin-Soy Dipping Sauce. Serves 4.

Mirin-Soy Dipping Sauce: In saucepan heat 3 tablespoons *mirin or dry sherry* till warm. Remove from heat and ignite with a match. Shake pan gently till flame dies. Stir in 1 cup *Dashi* (see recipe, page 54) *or Homemade Chicken Broth* (see recipe, page 54), 3 tablespoons *soy sauce,* and dash *salt.* Bring to boiling; cool.

Fried Shrimp Balls

1½ pounds fresh *or* frozen shrimp
⅓ cup finely chopped water
    chestnuts
2 tablespoons finely chopped
    onion
1 egg
¾ cup soft bread crumbs (1 slice)
2 tablespoons finely chopped,
    seeded, and rinsed canned
    green chili peppers
2 tablespoons snipped parsley
1 clove garlic, minced
¼ teaspoon ground turmeric
    All-purpose flour
    Cooking oil for deep-fat frying

Thaw shrimp, if frozen. Shell and devein shrimp. Pat dry with paper toweling. Cut shrimp into pieces. In small mixer bowl combine shrimp, water chestnuts, and onion; beat with electric mixer till well mashed. Add egg, bread crumbs, green chili peppers, parsley, garlic, turmeric, and ½ teaspoon *salt;* beat well. Shape mixture into balls, using about 2 tablespoonfuls for each. Roll the balls in flour to lightly coat.

Fry the balls, several at a time, in deep hot oil (365°) about 3 minutes or till golden brown. Remove balls using a slotted spoon or wire strainer. Drain on paper toweling. Keep warm while frying remaining balls. Serves 4 to 6.

Red-Cooked Fish, Szechwan-Style

2 12-ounce fresh *or* frozen dressed
    trout (with head and tail)
3 tablespoons soy sauce
2 tablespoons dry sherry
2 tablespoons grated gingerroot
    Cooking oil for deep-fat frying
6 green onions, bias-sliced into
    1½-inch lengths
2 cloves garlic, minced
1 tablespoon cooking oil
1 tablespoon hot bean sauce
1 tablespoon cornstarch
1 teaspoon sugar
1 cup cold water
    Hot cooked rice (optional)

Thaw fish, if frozen. Score each fish with about eight ⅛-inch-deep diagonal cuts on each side (this allows the seasonings to penetrate). For marinade, combine soy sauce, dry sherry, and gingerroot. Place fish in a shallow baking dish. Pour marinade over fish, making sure it penetrates all cuts. Let stand at room temperature for 20 minutes, turning fish over after 10 minutes. Drain fish, reserving marinade. Pat fish dry with paper toweling. Pour cooking oil into a large skillet to depth of ¾ inch; heat oil. Cook fish in hot oil 3 to 4 minutes. Turn fish and cook 3 to 4 minutes more or till fish flakes easily when tested with a fork. Drain fish on paper toweling; keep warm while preparing sauce.

To prepare sauce, in small saucepan cook onions and garlic in the 1 tablespoon hot oil till tender but not brown; stir in hot bean sauce. Combine cornstarch and sugar; blend in cold water and reserved marinade. Add to mixture in saucepan. Cook and stir till thickened and bubbly. Pour sauce over fish. Serve with hot cooked rice, if desired. Serves 4.

Stuffed Fish

4 fresh *or* frozen fish fillets
    (1½ pounds)
2 slices boiled ham
1 egg
¼ cup chopped onion
1 tablespoon soy sauce
1 teaspoon cornstarch
1 teaspoon grated gingerroot
½ teaspoon sugar
⅛ teaspoon pepper
½ cup finely chopped fresh spinach

Thaw fish, if frozen. Skin fillets, if necessary. Cut fish into eight 3x2-inch pieces, patching as necessary to make even pieces. Cut slices of ham into quarters. In a shallow bowl combine egg, onion, soy sauce, cornstarch, gingerroot, sugar, and pepper; mix well. Dip fish pieces into egg mixture. Place one piece of ham on each fish piece. Spread 1 tablespoon of spinach over ham. Fold fish over to enclose filling; secure with wooden picks.

Fry fish rolls, a few at a time, in deep hot oil (365°) for 2 to 3 minutes or till golden. Using slotted spoon or wire strainer, remove and drain on paper toweling. Keep warm while frying remaining fish rolls. Makes 4 to 6 servings.

Szechwan Lotus Root Meatballs

1 slightly beaten egg
½ cup finely chopped, peeled fresh
    lotus root *or* finely chopped
    canned lotus root
¼ cup thinly sliced green onion
1 tablespoon cornstarch
1 tablespoon soy sauce
1 teaspoon grated gingerroot *or*
    ¼ teaspoon ground ginger
¼ teaspoon salt
¼ teaspoon pepper *or* crushed
    Szechwan pepper
½ pound ground pork *or* ground
    beef
    Cooking oil for deep-fat frying

In large bowl combine egg, lotus root, green onion, cornstarch, soy sauce, gingerroot or ground ginger, salt, and pepper or Szechwan pepper. Add pork or beef; mix well.

Using a rounded teaspoon of meat mixture for each meatball, carefully drop several meatballs at a time into deep hot oil (365°). Cook 2 to 2½ minutes or till deep golden brown. Remove meatballs using a slotted spoon or wire strainer. Drain on paper toweling. Keep warm in 250° oven; fry remaining meatballs. Makes 30 meatballs.

Serving suggestion: Serve the meatballs on wooden picks as appetizers, or enjoy them as a main dish. Makes 3 main dish servings.

Shrimp Toast Appetizers

8 slices firm-textured white bread
1 4½-ounce can shrimp, drained
    and chopped
1 egg
1 tablespoon cornstarch
1 tablespoon finely chopped
    water chestnuts
1 tablespoon thinly sliced green
    onion
2 teaspoons soy sauce
1 teaspoon grated gingerroot
1 teaspoon dry sherry
½ teaspoon sugar
¼ teaspoon salt
    Cooking oil for deep-fat frying

With a serrated knife, trim crusts from bread slices (stack 4 slices for easier trimming). Lay the bread slices in a single layer on a cookie sheet; let stand 1 hour. Turn bread slices over; let stand 1 hour more. (If bread has been opened more than a day, this step is unnecessary.)

In a small mixer bowl combine shrimp and egg; beat at low speed of electric mixer for ½ minute, scraping sides of bowl constantly. Add cornstarch, water chestnuts, green onion, soy sauce, gingerroot, dry sherry, sugar, and salt; beat till well blended. Spread about 2 tablespoons shrimp mixture on each bread slice.

Cut each slice into 4 triangles. Fry bread triangles, a few at a time with shrimp side down, in deep hot oil (365°) for 30 seconds. Turn and fry 30 seconds more or till golden brown. Using a slotted spoon or wire strainer, remove toast from hot oil. Drain on paper toweling. Keep warm in 250° oven. Serve as soon as all triangles are fried. Makes 32 appetizers.

Korean Fried Beef Strips

1 pound beef flank steak *or* top
    round steak
2 tablespoons finely chopped
    onion *or* sliced green onion
2 tablespoons soy sauce
1 tablespoon cooking oil
½ teaspoon sugar
1 clove garlic, minced
⅛ teaspoon bottled hot pepper
    sauce
    Cooking oil for deep-fat frying
    Hot cooked rice
    Soy Dipping Sauce

Partially freeze beef; thinly slice across the grain into bite-size strips. In bowl combine onion, soy sauce, the 1 tablespoon oil, the sugar, garlic, and hot pepper sauce. Add beef strips, tossing to coat. Let stand 30 minutes at room temperature, stirring once or twice. Place some of the strips in a wire strainer or frying basket. Fry strips in deep hot oil (365°) for 30 to 45 seconds or just till browned. Drain on paper toweling. Keep fried strips warm in 250° oven. Repeat with remaining strips. Serve with rice and individual dishes of Soy Dipping Sauce. Makes 4 servings.

Soy Dipping Sauce: Combine 3 tablespoons *soy sauce;* 2 tablespoons *water;* 2 tablespoons *dry sherry;* 1 tablespoon sliced *green onion;* 2 teaspoons *sugar;* 1 teaspoon *sesame seed,* toasted; and a few dashes *bottled hot pepper sauce.*

Spiced Beef Short Ribs

2 cups water
½ cup chopped onion
¼ cup soy sauce
¼ cup dry sherry
4 slices gingerroot
2 star anise *or* 1 teaspoon
    crushed aniseed
2 cloves garlic, minced
1 teaspoon salt
1 teaspoon sugar
½ teaspoon pepper
½ teaspoon sesame oil
2 pounds beef chuck short ribs,
    sawed in half across bones
2 beaten eggs
¼ cup cornstarch *or* all-purpose
    flour
    Cooking oil for deep-fat frying

In large Dutch oven combine water, onion, soy sauce, dry sherry, gingerroot, star anise or aniseed, garlic, salt, sugar, pepper, and sesame oil; mix well. Cut ribs into two-rib portions. Trim excess fat from ribs. Add rib pieces to mixture in Dutch oven. Cover and simmer 1¼ to 1½ hours or till ribs are just tender. Drain ribs, reserving liquid. Cool ribs completely.

Stir together eggs and cornstarch or flour. Dip rib pieces in batter, swirling to coat evenly. Fry ribs, a few at a time, in deep hot oil (365°) about 4 minutes or till golden brown. Using a slotted spoon or wire strainer, remove ribs and drain on paper toweling. Makes 4 to 6 servings.

Skewered Beef and Mushrooms *Korean*

1 pound beef top round steak
¼ cup soy sauce
2 teaspoons sesame seed, toasted
    and crushed
2 teaspoons sesame oil
1 teaspoon sugar
1 clove garlic, minced
½ teaspoon salt
½ teaspoon crushed red pepper
    Dash pepper
    Boiling water
12 fresh mushrooms
4 green onions, bias sliced into
    2-inch lengths
    All-purpose flour
2 beaten eggs
½ cup cooking oil

Partially freeze beef; thinly slice across the grain into bite-size strips. Place beef in a shallow dish. Combine soy sauce, sesame seed, sesame oil, sugar, garlic, salt, crushed red pepper, and dash pepper. Pour the soy mixture over beef; let stand for 30 minutes, turning beef occasionally. Drain beef. Meanwhile, pour boiling water over mushrooms to cover. Let stand a few minutes; drain well and discard stems. On twelve short bamboo or metal skewers, thread beef strips accordion-style alternately with mushroom caps and green onion pieces. Roll each skewer in flour to coat thoroughly. Dip in beaten eggs.

In large skillet cook the skewers in hot oil for 2 to 3 minutes on each side or till meat is browned and vegetables are tender. Remove skewers from skillet; drain thoroughly on paper toweling. Makes 4 servings.

Slice Meat the Easy Way

Once you learn to slice meat thinly, you're well on your way to becoming a skilled Oriental cook. The trick to mastering this technique is to partially freeze the meat (or partially thaw frozen meat) and then thinly slice it across the grain. Allow 45 to 60 minutes to partially freeze a 1-inch-thick piece of meat. (See sketch on page 43 for how to hold the meat and cleaver or knife when slicing.)

Candied Fruit Slices

¾ **cup all-purpose flour**
½ **cup ice water**
1 **beaten egg**
2 **medium apples *or* firm bananas**
   Cooking oil for deep-fat frying
1 **cup sugar**
1 **cup light corn syrup**
½ **cup water**
2 **tablespoons cooking oil**
2 **teaspoons black sesame seeds**
   (optional)
   Ice water

In mixing bowl prepare batter by combining flour, the ½ cup ice water, and egg; beat smooth. Peel and core apples; cut into ⅜-inch-thick slices (or peel bananas and cut into 1-inch-thick chunks). Drop apples or bananas into prepared batter; turn to coat well. Fry apple slices or banana pieces, a few at a time, in the deep hot oil (365°) for 1 to 2 minutes or till lightly golden. Drain on paper toweling.

At serving time, prepare syrup by combining sugar, corn syrup, the ½ cup water, and the 2 tablespoons cooking oil in 1½-quart saucepan. Bring to boiling over medium heat; stir till sugar dissolves. Continue boiling, stirring occasionally, till mixture turns light caramel color (280° on candy thermometer). Stir in black sesame seeds, if desired. Immediately turn heat to *low*. Working very quickly, dip fruit pieces in hot syrup to coat, then *drop* into a large bowl of ice water. Remove at once to buttered serving platter. Serve immediately as the candy glaze will soften if allowed to stand (there will be left-over syrup). Makes 4 to 6 servings.

Clean-up suggestion: Fill the syrup-coated saucepan with water and heat till syrup melts sufficiently to clean pan.

Date-Filled Wontons

1 **8-ounce package (1⅓ cups)**
   finely snipped pitted dates
⅓ **cup granulated sugar**
¼ **cup water**
½ **cup finely chopped walnuts**
2 **tablespoons lemon juice *or***
   orange juice
½ **teaspoon vanilla**
40 **wonton skins *or* 10 egg roll**
   skins, cut in quarters
   Cooking oil for deep-fat frying
   Sifted powdered sugar

To prepare the date filling, in small saucepan combine dates, granulated sugar, and water; bring to boil. Cook, stirring constantly, over low heat about 4 minutes or till thickened. Remove from heat; stir in walnuts, lemon or orange juice, and vanilla. Cool date filling.

Position skin with one point toward you. Spread 1 teaspoon of filling just off center of skin. Fold bottom point of wonton skin over filling; tuck point under filling. Roll up wonton into log so that filling is completely enclosed; wet point and press to seal. Wet the inside of each end of roll; twist ends to seal. Repeat with remaining skins and filling.

Fry wontons, a few at a time, in deep hot oil (365°) for 1½ to 2 minutes or till golden. Drain on paper toweling. Cool. Dust with powdered sugar. Makes 40.

Chinese New Year Cakes

1½ **cups all-purpose flour**
¼ **cup sugar**
2 **teaspoons baking powder**
2 **beaten eggs**
⅓ **cup water *or* milk**
1 **tablespoon cooking oil**
1 **1⅞-ounce can sesame seed**
   (about ⅓ cup)
   Cooking oil for deep-fat frying

Combine flour, sugar, baking powder, and ½ teaspoon *salt*. Stir together eggs, water or milk, and the 1 tablespoon cooking oil. Add flour mixture all at once and stir just till moistened. Drop batter by tablespoonfuls into bowl of sesame seed; turn to coat. Place sesame-coated cakes on waxed paper. Let stand 15 minutes. Fry, several at a time, in deep hot oil (365°) for 2½ to 3 minutes or till puffy and golden. Drain on paper toweling. Serve warm. Makes 20.

Date-Filled Wontons or *Candied Fruit Slices* are perfect accompaniments for any dinner party.

Firepot

1 pound beef top round *or* sirloin steak
1 tablespoon cornstarch
1 tablespoon soy sauce
2 ounces bean threads
½ pound fresh *or* frozen large shrimp
8 ounces fresh tofu (bean curd)
1½ cups fresh mushrooms
4 to 6 charcoal briquettes
8 cups Homemade Chicken Broth (see recipe, page 54)
4 cups sliced Chinese cabbage
2 cups small fresh spinach leaves
6 green onions, bias-sliced into 1-inch lengths
Oyster Sauce, Chinese Mustard, and Ginger Soy (see recipes, pages 84 and 85)

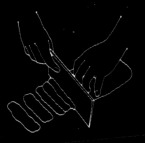

Slice beef thinly across the grain into bite-size strips.

Partially freeze beef; thinly slice across the grain into bite-size strips, as shown. Sprinkle beef with cornstarch and soy sauce. Using your hands, work the seasonings into the meat.

In a large bowl pour hot water over bean threads to cover; let stand 30 minutes. Drain well; squeeze out excess moisture. Cut bean threads into 2-inch lengths.

Thaw shrimp, if frozen. Shell shrimp; cut down back and use a knife to remove vein, as shown. Halve shrimp lengthwise. Cut tofu into 2x¼-inch strips. Halve mushrooms.

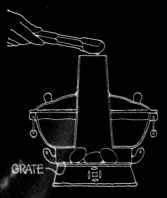

Use a sharp knife to cut down back of shrimp and with its point scrape out the vein.

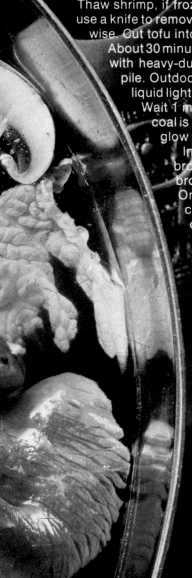

About 30 minutes before serving, line a heatproof pan with heavy-duty foil; place charcoal briquettes in a pile. Outdoors or in a well ventilated area, drizzle liquid lighter over the entire surface of briquettes. Wait 1 minute, then ignite with a match. (Charcoal is ready to use when flame dies down to a glow and no areas of black show.)

In large saucepan bring the chicken broth to boiling. Pour the hot chicken broth into the firepot. Cover the firepot. One at a time, carefully place the hot charcoal briquettes down the chimney of the firepot and rest them on the grate, as shown. Remove the firepot cover. (Or, use a metal fondue pot instead of a firepot. Pour broth into metal fondue pot till about half full; heat to boiling on range top. Transfer to fondue burner.) Add an assortment of meat, shrimp, and vegetables to the hot broth. Replace the firepot cover, as shown. Cook till meat and shrimp are done and vegetables are tender. Using small wire baskets, chopsticks, or fork, remove food. Dip cooked food in desired sauce. Repeat with remaining ingredients until all are cooked. Makes 6 to 8 servings.

Serving suggestion: In the remaining broth cook fine noodles and serve as a soup.

GRATE

Using tongs, place the hot charcoal briquettes down the firepot's chimney and rest them on the grate.

After adding food to hot broth in firepot, replace its metal cover.

Red Simmered Pork Cubes

1 tablespoon grated gingerroot
1 teaspoon sugar
2 cloves garlic, minced
2 tablespoons cooking oil
1 pound boneless pork, cut into
    ¾-inch pieces
½ cup chopped onion
1 cup water
2 tablespoons soy sauce
2 tablespoons dry sherry
½ teaspoon salt
1 star anise *or* ½ teaspoon aniseed
1 cup thinly sliced fresh
    mushrooms *or* 1 4½-ounce jar
    sliced mushrooms
½ cup thinly sliced bamboo shoots

In skillet cook gingerroot, sugar, and garlic in hot oil for 30 seconds or till sugar and garlic turn light brown. Add pork and onion; cook and stir till pork is browned on all sides. Combine water, soy sauce, dry sherry, salt, and star anise or aniseed. Pour mixture into skillet. Simmer, covered, for 30 minutes. Stir in the sliced mushrooms and bamboo shoots. Simmer mixture, covered, about 15 minutes more. Makes 4 to 6 servings.

Simmered Pork with Spinach *Japanese*

¾ pound boneless pork
1 cup grated Chinese white radish
    or radish
¾ cup sake
2 tablespoons soy sauce
1 tablespoon grated gingerroot
¼ teaspoon salt
1 cup sliced fresh mushrooms
4 cups small fresh spinach leaves
6 green onions, bias-sliced into
    1-inch lengths
1 tablespoon cornstarch

Partially freeze pork; thinly slice. Place grated radish in a double layer of paper toweling; press tightly to extract as much moisture as possible. Set aside.

In large skillet combine sake, soy sauce, gingerroot, salt, and 2 tablespoons *water*. Add pork and mushrooms. Simmer, covered, for 10 minutes or till pork is tender: turn pork slices occasionally. Stir in spinach leaves and green onion. Cook, covered, for 2 to 3 minutes.

Remove pork and vegetables and arrange on heated serving platter. For sauce, measure 1 cup cooking liquid. Slowly blend 1 tablespoon cold *water* into cornstarch; stir into cooking liquid. Cook and stir till thickened and bubbly. Pass sauce. Garnish with grated radish. Makes 4 to 6 servings.

Spareribs Simmered with Mushrooms *Korean*

4 dried mushrooms *or* ½ cup sliced
    fresh mushrooms
2 pounds meaty pork spareribs,
    sawed in half across bones
2 teaspoons grated gingerroot
2 cloves garlic, minced
1 tablespoon cooking oil
¾ cup water
2 tablespoons sliced green onion
2 tablespoons soy sauce
2 tablespoons sake *or* dry sherry
2 teaspoons sesame seed, toasted
1 teaspoon sugar
2 tablespoons cold water
4 teaspoons cornstarch
1 tablespoon sliced green onion

In small bowl soak dried mushrooms (not fresh mushrooms) in enough hot water to cover for 30 minutes; squeeze to drain well. Slice mushrooms into thin strips; discard stems.

Cut spareribs into 2- or 3-rib portions. In large heavy skillet cook gingerroot and garlic in hot oil for 30 seconds. Add sparerib pieces and cook 3 to 4 minutes or till browned on all sides. Drain excess fat. Combine mushrooms, the ¾ cup water, 2 tablespoons green onion, soy sauce, sake or dry sherry, sesame seed, and sugar; pour atop spareribs. Simmer, covered, 40 to 45 minutes or till spareribs are tender.

Remove spareribs and place on heated serving platter; keep warm. Slowly blend the 2 tablespoons cold water into cornstarch. Stir into hot mixture. Cook and stir till thickened and bubbly. Pour over spareribs. Sprinkle with 1 tablespoon sliced green onion to garnish. Makes 4 servings.

Lion's Head

1 **slightly beaten egg**
1 **4-ounce can chopped mushrooms, drained**
¼ **cup fine dry bread crumbs**
¼ **cup thinly sliced green onion**
¼ **cup finely chopped water chestnuts**
1 **tablespoon soy sauce**
2 **teaspoons cornstarch**
1 **to 2 teaspoons grated gingerroot**
½ **teaspoon sugar**
¼ **teaspoon salt**
⅛ **teaspoon pepper**
1 **pound ground pork** *or* **ground beef**
2 **tablespoons cooking oil**
2 **cups Homemade Chicken Broth (see recipe, page 54)**
2 **tablespoons dry sherry**
2 **tablespoons soy sauce**
1 **medium head Chinese cabbage, sliced 1 inch wide (6 cups)**
2 **tablespoons cold water**
2 **tablespoons cornstarch**

In bowl combine egg, mushrooms, bread crumbs, green onion, water chestnuts, the 1 tablespoon soy sauce, the 2 teaspoons cornstarch, gingerroot, sugar, salt, and pepper. Add ground pork or beef; mix well. Shape into six meatballs. In skillet or Dutch oven cook meatballs in hot oil 4 to 5 minutes, turning meatballs frequently to evenly brown all sides. Remove meatballs from hot oil; drain on paper toweling.

Remove oil; wipe skillet or Dutch oven clean with paper toweling. Combine chicken broth, dry sherry, and the 2 tablespoons soy sauce; heat to boiling. Add meatballs. Simmer, covered, for 35 minutes. Top with sliced Chinese cabbage. Simmer, covered, 5 minutes more. Using slotted spoon or wire strainer, remove cabbage and meatballs and drain well; reserve 2 cups of the cooking broth. Arrange drained cabbage on heated serving platter and top with meatballs. Blend the cold water into the 2 tablespoons cornstarch. Stir into hot broth. Cook and stir till thickened and bubbly. Pour some of the sauce atop meatballs. Pass the remaining sauce. Makes 6 servings.

Eating with Chopsticks

Before your next Oriental party, try this simple practice with chopsticks or pencils to impress guests with your chopstick dexterity. Place one chopstick, about two-thirds of its length from the narrow tip, in the hollow between the base of the thumb and index finger. Let the chopstick rest on the end of the ring finger or little finger. Close the base of the thumb over the chopstick to hold it securely. In the same hand hold the second chopstick firmly between the tip of the thumb and the index finger, with the middle finger resting on the first chopstick as shown. Hold the chopsticks about an inch apart and parallel to each other. To pick up food, the index and middle fingers move the chopstick with the thumb steadying it. You move only the top chopstick as indicated by the arrow; the bottom one remains stationary. Hold the chopsticks at an angle to the plate and pick up food with the narrow tips. While eating, occasionally tap the ends of the chopsticks to keep the tips even.

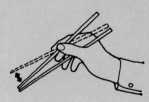

Curried Beef

1 **small onion, thinly sliced and
    separated into rings**
2 **cloves garlic, minced**
2 **tablespoons cooking oil**
1 **pound beef round steak, cut in
    ¾-inch pieces**
1 **cup water**
2 **tablespoons dry sherry**
1 **tablespoon instant beef bouillon
    granules**
2 **teaspoons curry powder**
1 **teaspoon sugar**
1 **teaspoon grated gingerroot**
1 **tablespoon cold water**
1 **tablespoon cornstarch**
2 **medium tomatoes, peeled,
    seeded, and chopped**

In large skillet cook onion and garlic in hot oil till onion is tender but not brown. Add beef and cook quickly till all sides are browned. Drain off excess fat. Stir in the 1 cup water, dry sherry, bouillon granules, curry powder, sugar, gingerroot, and dash *salt*. Bring to boiling. Simmer, covered, 35 to 40 minutes or till beef is tender. Slowly blend the 1 tablespoon cold water into cornstarch; stir into hot mixture. Cook and stir till thickened and bubbly. Stir in tomatoes; heat through. Serve over hot cooked rice, if desired. Makes 4 servings.

Short Ribs in Black Bean Sauce

1 **tablespoon fermented black
    beans**
¼ **cup finely chopped onion**
1 **tablespoon dry sherry**
1 **tablespoon soy sauce**
1 **teaspoon sugar**
2 **cloves garlic, minced**
3 **pounds beef plate *or* chuck short
    ribs, sawed in half across
    bones**
2 **tablespoons cooking oil**
1 **cup water**

Rinse black beans under cold running water; drain well. Using a fork, mash beans. Combine beans, onion, dry sherry, soy sauce, sugar, and garlic. Set aside. In a large heavy skillet or Dutch oven brown ribs in hot oil, turning ribs to brown all sides. Drain excess fat. Add black bean mixture and the water. Bring to boiling. Simmer, covered, 1½ to 2 hours or till ribs are tender. Spoon off excess fat. Makes 4 servings.

Braised Beef with Vegetables

8 **dried lily buds (optional)**
2 **tablespoons soy sauce**
2 **teaspoons grated gingerroot**
½ **teaspoon Homemade Five Spice
    Powder (see recipe, page 31)**
1 **clove garlic, minced**
1 **pound beef round steak, cut in
    ¾-inch pieces**
2 **tablespoons cooking oil**
4 **teaspoons instant beef bouillon
    granules**
1 **cup bias-sliced carrots**
1 **8-ounce can bamboo shoots,
    drained and halved lengthwise**
1 **6-ounce package frozen pea
    pods, thawed**
3 **tablespoons cornstarch**

In small bowl soak lily buds in enough hot water to cover for 30 minutes; drain. Slice each lily bud into 1-inch lengths; discard tough stem ends.

For marinade combine soy sauce, gingerroot, five spice powder, and garlic; add to beef. Using your hands, mix the seasonings thoroughly into meat. Marinate the meat for 15 minutes at room temperature.

In large skillet cook meat in hot oil till browned. Drain excess fat. Combine bouillon granules and 2 cups hot *water;* stir to dissolve granules. Add the bouillon, lily buds, and carrots to beef. Bring to boiling; reduce heat. Simmer, covered, 35 to 40 minutes or till meat is tender. Add bamboo shoots and pea pods. Simmer 2 minutes more or till beef and vegetables are tender. Slowly blend 3 tablespoons cold *water* into cornstarch; stir into hot mixture. Cook and stir till thickened and bubbly. Serve with hot cooked noodles or rice, if desired. Makes 4 to 6 servings.

Oriental Beef

1½ pounds beef stew meat
1 tablespoon cooking oil
½ cup chopped onion
½ cup dry white wine
¼ cup soy sauce
1 clove garlic, minced
2 teaspoons sugar
½ teaspoon ground ginger
1 16-ounce can tomato wedges
1 6-ounce package frozen pea
   pods
1 3-ounce can sliced mushrooms,
   drained
2 tablespoons cornstarch

Cut meat into 1-inch cubes. In large skillet brown meat in hot oil. Remove from heat. Add the onion, wine, soy sauce, garlic, sugar, ginger, and 1 cup *water*. Cover and simmer 1½ hours. Add undrained tomatoes, frozen pea pods, and mushrooms. Bring to boiling; cook and stir, uncovered, 2 to 3 minutes or till pea pods are crisp-tender. Slowly blend ½ cup cold *water* into cornstarch; stir into hot mixture. Cook and stir till thickened and bubbly. Serve over hot cooked rice, if desired. Makes 6 servings.

Red-Cooked Chicken

1½ cups water
1 cup soy sauce
8 green onions, bias-sliced into
   1½-inch lengths
¼ cup dry sherry
2 tablespoons brown sugar
2 teaspoons grated gingerroot
1 clove garlic, minced
1 star anise, crushed, *or* ½
   teaspoon aniseed, crushed
1 3½- to 4-pound whole
   broiler-fryer chicken

In large kettle or Dutch oven combine water, soy sauce, green onions, dry sherry, brown sugar, gingerroot, garlic, and star anise or aniseed; mix well. Place chicken in mixture. Cover; bring to boiling. Reduce heat; simmer 25 minutes. Using tongs, turn chicken over. Cover; simmer 25 to 30 minutes more or till chicken is tender, basting frequently with the cooking liquid during the last 10 minutes.

Remove chicken from pan, reserving broth. Using a sharp cleaver or knife, chop chicken, bones and all, into bite-size sections. Reassemble chicken to its original whole shape (refer to tip box on page 77). Or, cut the chicken into quarters. Strain broth to remove green onions; skim excess fat. Pass some of the broth. Serve chicken with Soft Fried Noodles, if desired (see recipe, page 81). Makes 6 servings.

Wine-Basted Chicken

1 5- to 6-pound stewing chicken,
   cut up, *or* 2 3-pound
   broiler-fryer chickens, cut up
4 cups water
1 cup dry white wine
4 stalks celery with leaves, cut up
1 small onion, cut up
2 star anise, crushed, *or* 1
   teaspoon aniseed, crushed
½ teaspoon salt
   Honey-Oyster Sauce *or* Sweet
   Lemon Sauce

Place chicken in large kettle or Dutch oven; add water, white wine, celery, onion, star anise or aniseed, and salt. Cover; bring to boiling. Simmer about 1 hour for broiler-fryers *or* 2 to 2½ hours for stewing chicken or till tender. Remove chicken; discard broth. Set chicken aside to cool. When chicken is cool enough to handle, remove meat, discarding bones and skin. Chill chicken thoroughly. Thinly slice chicken; arrange on serving platter. Pass Honey-Oyster Sauce or Sweet Lemon Sauce. Serves 6 to 8.

Honey-Oyster Sauce: In a small bowl combine ¼ cup *honey*, 2 tablespoons *Oyster Sauce* (see recipe, page 85), 2 tablespoons *soy sauce*, 1 tablespoon *water*, and 1 teaspoon grated *gingerroot*. Let stand 30 minutes before serving.

Sweet Lemon Sauce: In a small bowl combine 3 tablespoons *catsup*, 2 tablespoons *brown sugar*, 1 teaspoon grated *lemon peel*, 2 tablespoons *lemon juice*, 1 tablespoon *water*, 1 tablespoon *soy sauce*, and 1 teaspoon *vinegar;* mix well. Let stand 30 minutes before serving.

Duck with Dried Chestnuts

1 4- to 5-pound domestic duckling
    or 1 3- to 4-pound whole
      roasting chicken
½ cup dried chestnuts
¼ cup finely chopped onion
2 tablespoons soy sauce
2 tablespoons dry sherry
1 tablespoon hot bean sauce
1 teaspoon sugar
1 teaspoon grated gingerroot
1 clove garlic, minced
2 green onions, bias-sliced into
    1-inch lengths

Rinse bird and pat dry; rub cavity with *salt*. Place duck or chicken in a large kettle or Dutch oven; add 1 cup *water*. Stir in chestnuts, onion, soy sauce, dry sherry, hot bean sauce, sugar, gingerroot, and garlic. Bring mixture to boiling. Simmer, covered, for 1¾ to 2 hours or till meat is tender; turn bird over the last 30 minutes of cooking. Using a sharp cleaver or knife, chop duck or chicken into bite-size sections, bones and all. Reassemble to original whole shape (refer to tip box on page 77). (*Or,* carve whole bird.) Spoon excess fat from cooking sauce; pour some of the sauce over duck or chicken. Garnish with green onion. Makes 3 or 4 servings.

Ginger Chicken with Lily Buds

20 dried lily buds
1 tablespoon grated gingerroot
2 cloves garlic, minced
2 tablespoons cooking oil
1 2- to 2½-pound broiler-fryer
    chicken, cut up
3 tablespoons dry sherry
3 tablespoons soy sauce
2 teaspoons honey
½ teaspoon dry mustard
½ teaspoon Szechwan pepper *or*
    whole black peppercorns,
    crushed
½ of a star anise, crushed, *or* ¼
    teaspoon aniseed, crushed

Soak dried lily buds in enough hot water to cover for 30 minutes; drain. Cut off and discard stem ends. Halve the lily buds crosswise.

    In large skillet cook gingerroot and garlic in hot oil about 30 seconds. Add chicken pieces and brown about 15 minutes, turning frequently. Drain excess fat. Combine drained lily buds, dry sherry, soy sauce, honey, dry mustard, crushed pepper, star anise or aniseed, and 1 tablespoon *water*; add to the skillet. Cover; simmer over low heat about 35 minutes, stirring occasionally. Remove chicken to serving platter. Spoon excess fat from broth. Pour broth over chicken. Makes 4 servings.

Lemon Squabs

2 12- to 14-ounce squabs *or* 2
    1-pound Cornish game hens
2 tablespoons dark soy sauce
½ cup cooking oil
⅓ cup water
2 tablespoons sugar
2 tablespoons lemon juice
1 teaspoon light soy sauce
½ teaspoon cognac *or* brandy
¼ teaspoon sesame oil
    Halved lemon slices
    Green onion brushes

Rub birds inside and out with dark soy sauce. In wok or skillet brown birds on all sides in hot cooking oil about 10 minutes or till golden. Drain excess fat. Combine water, sugar, lemon juice, light soy sauce, cognac or brandy, and sesame oil. Add to wok or skillet. Reduce heat; cover and simmer 45 to 50 minutes or till birds are tender. Remove birds; drain on paper toweling. Keep warm. Over high heat, boil pan juices about 5 minutes or till reduced to ¼ cup liquid. Using a sharp cleaver or knife, chop birds into bite-size sections, bones and all. Reassemble to original whole shape (refer to tip box on page 77). Arrange on platter. Spoon pan juices over birds. Garnish with lemon and green onion. Makes 2 servings.

    Serving suggestion: Serve the birds with shrimp or lobster chips from an Oriental shop. Fry chips in deep hot oil according to package directions. (Store unfried chips in a tightly sealed plastic bag.)

Colorful deep-fried shrimp chips and green onion brushes add a festive touch to the soy-glazed *Lemon Squabs*.

Tea Leaf Eggs *(pictured on page 2)*

8 to 10 eggs
2 tablespoons soy sauce
4 teaspoons aniseed
2 inches stick cinnamon
2 teaspoons black tea leaves
1 teaspoon sugar
1 teaspoon salt

In saucepan cover eggs with cold water to a depth of at least 1 inch above eggs. Rapidly bring to boiling; cover pan tightly. Reduce heat; simmer 15 minutes. Rinse quickly in cold water till eggs are cool enough to handle; drain. Tap eggs gently all over till shells are a network of fine cracks (do not remove shells). Return eggs to saucepan; add soy sauce, aniseed, stick cinnamon, black tea, sugar, salt, and 2 cups cold *water*. Bring to boiling; reduce heat. Simmer, covered, about 2 hours (add boiling water to keep eggs covered, if needed). Drain; chill eggs well. Before serving, roll eggs between palms of hands to loosen shell. Peel, starting from large end of egg. Makes 8 to 10.

Yosenabe *Japanese* *(pictured on page 56)*

6 dried mushrooms
1 2-ounce package bean thread
4 ounces fresh *or* frozen rock cod *or* other fish
2 cups coarsely chopped Chinese cabbage
2 cups fresh spinach (6 ounces)
6 large shrimp in shells
1 cup shucked oysters
6 cherrystone clams in shells, washed
6 slices fish cake (kamaboko) (optional)
4 ounces fresh tofu (bean curd), cut into 1½-inch pieces
4 green onions, bias-sliced into 1-inch lengths
4 cups Dashi (see recipe, page 54)

Cover dried mushrooms with warm water; soak 30 minutes. Cover bean thread with warm water; soak 15 minutes. Drain mushrooms and bean thread well and set aside. Thaw fish, if frozen. Put fish in colander or deep-fry basket; blanch by plunging into boiling water and cooking for 3 minutes. Immediately plunge into cold water; cool. Drain. Repeat blanching procedure with Chinese cabbage and spinach. In large deep skillet arrange mushrooms, bean thread, fish, Chinese cabbage, spinach, shrimp, oysters, clams, fish cake, tofu, and onions. Heat dashi to boiling; pour over ingredients in skillet. Cover and cook 10 minutes. Serve in bowls. Makes 6 servings.

Planning an Oriental-Style Meal

If you enjoy cooking, you'll love planning an Oriental meal. Instead of limiting the menu to one main dish, it's typical to serve several main dishes and let the diners sample everything. As a guideline, plan to serve one main dish for every two people. (The number of servings given with each recipe in this book is for American-style meals where only one main dish is served. So, a recipe that "makes 4 servings" will actually make 6 to 8 Oriental-style servings.) See page 92 for additional menu planning information and several menus using recipes from this book.

Red-Cooked Fish with Pork Stuffing

1 2- to 2½-pound fresh *or* frozen
   dressed pike, perch, *or* red
   snapper (with head and tail)
2 tablespoons finely chopped
   onion
1½ teaspoons soy sauce
1 teaspoon cornstarch
½ teaspoon grated gingerroot
¼ teaspoon sugar
¼ pound ground pork
2 cups Homemade Chicken Broth
   (see recipe, page 54)
¼ cup dry sherry
¼ cup soy sauce
1 tablespoon grated gingerroot
1 clove garlic, minced
1 teaspoon sugar
6 green onions, bias-sliced into
   1½-inch lengths

Thaw fish, if frozen. To prepare the stuffing, in bowl combine finely chopped onion, the 1½ teaspoons soy sauce, cornstarch, the ½ teaspoon gingerroot, and the ¼ teaspoon sugar. Add ground pork; mix well.

Score fish with about six diagonal cuts on each side, slicing almost through to the bone. Sprinkle fish inside and out with *salt*. Fill fish cavity with the pork stuffing, patting stuffing to flatten evenly. Place fish on foil harness (see tip box on page 62) or place on greased rack of fish poacher. Lower into large kettle or fish poacher. Combine chicken broth, sherry, the ¼ cup soy sauce, the 1 tablespoon gingerroot, garlic, and the 1 teaspoon sugar. Pour over fish. Top fish with green onions. Cover and simmer 20 minutes or till fish flakes easily when tested with fork and stuffing is done. Remove fish to serving platter; spoon a little of the cooking liquid over fish. Makes 4 or 5 servings.

Whitefish in Sake-Flavored Sauce *Japanese*

1 16-ounce package frozen fish
   fillets, thawed
1½ cups sake
¼ cup soy sauce
2 tablespoons sugar
1 9-ounce package frozen whole
   green beans, thawed

Cut thawed fish into eight equal pieces. In large skillet combine sake, soy sauce, and sugar; bring to boiling. Halve green beans crosswise; add to sake mixture in skillet. Cover and cook 5 minutes. Add fish pieces; cover and cook 5 minutes more or till fish flakes easily when tested with a fork. With slotted spoon, remove fish pieces and green beans to warm serving platter. Drizzle ½ *cup* of the cooking liquid over fish and beans. Makes 4 servings.

Fish Simmered in Miso Sauce *Japanese*

1 16-ounce package frozen fish
   fillets, thawed
   Salt
¾ cup Dashi (see recipe, page 54)
   or Homemade Chicken Broth
   (see recipe, page 54)
1 tablespoon red miso (red bean
   paste)
2 tablespoons sake
1 teaspoon sugar
1 teaspoon rice wine vinegar *or*
   vinegar
1 teaspoon soy sauce
½ teaspoon grated gingerroot
1 green onion

Sprinkle fish lightly with salt. Cut fish fillets diagonally into 2x1-inch pieces.

To prepare stock, in a large heavy skillet blend dashi or chicken broth into red miso; add sake, sugar, rice vinegar or vinegar, soy sauce, and gingerroot. Bring stock to boiling, stirring to dissolve sugar. Reduce heat. Carefully add all the fish pieces to hot stock. Simmer fish, covered, for 8 to 10 minutes or till fish flakes easily when tested with a fork.

Cut green onion into three pieces. Slice pieces lengthwise into very thin strips. Place fish on heated serving platter. Pour some of the cooking stock over fish. Garnish with green onion strips. Makes 4 servings.

Rock Cod with Cashews

4 **cups Homemade Chicken Broth (see recipe, page 54)**
1 **cup sliced celery with tops**
½ **cup dry sherry**
1 **small onion, sliced and separated into rings**
1 **carrot, sliced**
6 **slices gingerroot**
6 **whole peppercorns**
1 **teaspoon salt**
1 **3-pound fresh *or* frozen dressed rock cod *or* red snapper (with head and tail)**
½ **cup cashews, broken into halves**
2 **tablespoons cooking oil**
2 **tablespoons soy sauce**
1 **teaspoon sesame oil**
4 **green onions, bias-sliced into 1½-inch lengths**
   Hot cooked rice
   Chinese parsley *or* parsley

In large kettle, Dutch oven, or fish poacher, bring the chicken broth to boiling. Add celery, sherry, onion, carrot, gingerroot, peppercorns, and salt. Simmer for 5 minutes. Place fish on foil harness (see tip box on page 62) or place on greased rack of fish poacher (if using kettle or Dutch oven, cut fish in half crosswise to fit). Lower fish into broth. Allow liquid to return to gentle boil. Simmer, covered, about 15 minutes or till fish flakes easily when tested with a fork. Carefully lift fish from liquid. Allow fish to drain briefly before placing on heated serving platter. If desired, reserve liquid (see note below).

Meanwhile, in small skillet stir-fry cashews in hot cooking oil for 2 minutes or till light golden brown. Spoon cashews and hot oil over fish. Combine soy sauce and sesame oil; drizzle over fish. Sprinkle with green onions. Serve with hot cooked rice. Garnish platter with sprigs of Chinese parsley or parsley (if fish has been halved, arrange garnish to conceal cut). Makes 6 servings.

Note: The flavorful cooking liquid is delicious used in soups. Simply strain the liquid by pouring it into a double thickness of cheesecloth or a clean cloth in a sieve set over a large bowl; let drain. Discard vegetables. Cover and refrigerate the liquid for up to two days.

When ready to use, heat the liquid to boiling. Stir in 8 ounces fresh *tofu* (bean curd), diced; heat through. Sprinkle with sliced *green onion*. (*Or,* stir in 2 cups diced, peeled *winter melon.* Simmer for 15 to 20 minutes or till melon is tender.) Makes 6 servings.

Crab and Asparagus Soup

2 **10½-ounce cans cut asparagus**
3 **cups Homemade Chicken Broth (see recipe, page 54)**
1 **4-ounce can sliced mushrooms**
1 **medium onion, coarsely chopped**
1 **tablespoon cornstarch**
1 **7½-ounce can crab meat, drained, flaked, and cartilage removed**
   Sliced green onion

Drain asparagus, reserving liquid. In saucepan combine reserved asparagus liquid, chicken broth, undrained mushrooms, and chopped onion. Cover and simmer till onion is tender, about 5 minutes. Slowly blend 2 tablespoons cold *water* into cornstarch. Stir into broth mixture; cook and stir till mixture thickens and bubbles. Stir in asparagus and crab meat; heat through. Sprinkle each serving with sliced green onion. Makes 6 servings.

Easy Corn and Egg-Shred Soup

1 **17-ounce can cream-style corn**
1 **10½-ounce can condensed chicken broth**
1 **5-ounce can boned chicken, coarsely chopped**
2 **eggs**
   Snipped fresh chives

In saucepan combine cream-style corn, the chicken broth, chicken, ½ cup *water,* and dash *pepper.* Heat to boiling, stirring occasionally. Beat eggs thoroughly. Pour slowly into the hot soup in a thin stream, beating constantly with a fork till egg cooks and shreds very finely. Ladle into soup bowls. Sprinkle fresh chives over each serving. Garnish with parsley sprigs, if desired. Makes 4 or 5 servings.

For fish at its delicate, flavorful best, simmer it briefly, as in *Rock Cod with Cashews.*

Homemade Chicken Broth

1 5- to 6-pound stewing chicken,
   cut up *or* 2 2½- to 3-pound
   broiler-fryer chickens, cut up
4 stalks celery with leaves, cut up
1 small onion, cut up
10 whole black peppercorns *or* ¼
   teaspoon pepper
3 sprigs parsley *or* fresh coriander
2 slices gingerroot
2 teaspoons salt

In 5-quart Dutch oven combine chicken and enough water to cover (about 6 cups). Add celery, onion, peppercorns or pepper, parsley or coriander, gingerroot, and salt. Cover; bring to boiling. Reduce heat; simmer 2 to 2½ hours for stewing chicken or about 1 hour for broiler-fryer chickens, or till chicken is tender. Remove chicken; strain broth. Set chicken and broth aside to cool.

When chicken is cool enough to handle, remove meat, discarding the skin and bones. Store chicken and broth separately in tightly covered containers in the refrigerator. Lift fat from broth when chilled. (Broth and chicken may be frozen separately in 1-cup portions. Use the meat in your favorite recipes calling for cooked chicken.) Use broth as directed in recipes. Makes 4 cups broth and 4 cups cooked chicken.

Ingredient substitution: When recipe calls for Homemade Chicken Broth, you can substitute canned chicken broth or make bouillon (1 teaspoon instant chicken bouillon granules for each 1 cup boiling water).

Dashi [Basic Soup Stock]

6 cups water
1 3-inch square dried kelp (kombu)
½ cup dried flaked bonito
   (katsuobushi)

In large saucepan bring water to boiling. Meanwhile, wash dried kelp under cold water. Add to the water in saucepan as it comes to a boil. Stir and let boil gently for 3 minutes. Remove kelp from the water and discard. Stir in dried flaked bonito; simmer for 10 minutes. Remove from the heat and do not disturb for 2 minutes to allow the flakes to settle to the bottom.

Place a double thickness of cheesecloth or other clean cloth in a sieve set over a large bowl. Pour in the stock and let the bonito drain; discard bonito. (Dashi is best if freshly prepared each time. It can also be cooled to room temperature and then stored, covered, in the refrigerator for up to 2 days.) Use as directed in recipes. Makes 5 cups.

Ingredient substitution: You can use instant dashi no moto prepared according to package directions in place of homemade Dashi.

Winter Melon Soup

6 dried mushrooms
3 cups diced, peeled winter melon
2 cups water
1¾ cups Homemade Chicken Broth
   (see recipe, above)
1 8-ounce can straw mushrooms,
   drained
1 large whole chicken breast,
   skinned, split, boned, and
   thinly sliced
   Salt
   Pepper

In bowl add enough hot water to dried mushrooms to cover. Soak 30 minutes; squeeze to drain well. Cut up mushrooms, discarding stems. In large saucepan combine winter melon, the 2 cups water, chicken broth, and the drained dried mushrooms. Cover and simmer for 20 to 25 minutes or till winter melon is tender. Add straw mushrooms and chicken slices. Cook, uncovered, 1 to 2 minutes more or till chicken is tender. Season to taste with salt and pepper. Makes 6 to 8 servings.

Hot and Sour Soup

- ½ pound boneless pork
- 3 tablespoons soy sauce
- 8 dried lily buds
- 4 dried mushrooms
- 4 dried tree ears
- 6 cups Homemade Chicken Broth (see recipe, page 54)
- 3 tablespoons rice wine vinegar *or* white vinegar
- ½ teaspoon pepper
- 8 ounces fresh tofu (bean curd)
- 1 tablespoon cold water
- 1 tablespoon cornstarch
- 1 beaten egg
- 2 tablespoons thinly sliced green onion

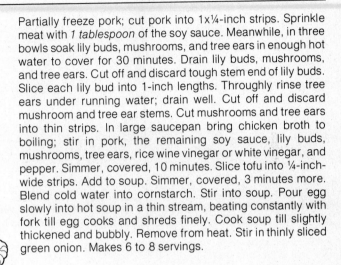

Partially freeze pork; cut pork into 1x¼-inch strips. Sprinkle meat with *1 tablespoon* of the soy sauce. Meanwhile, in three bowls soak lily buds, mushrooms, and tree ears in enough hot water to cover for 30 minutes. Drain lily buds, mushrooms, and tree ears. Cut off and discard tough stem end of lily buds. Slice each lily bud into 1-inch lengths. Throughly rinse tree ears under running water; drain well. Cut off and discard mushroom and tree ear stems. Cut mushrooms and tree ears into thin strips. In large saucepan bring chicken broth to boiling; stir in pork, the remaining soy sauce, lily buds, mushrooms, tree ears, rice wine vinegar or white vinegar, and pepper. Simmer, covered, 10 minutes. Slice tofu into ¼-inch-wide strips. Add to soup. Simmer, covered, 3 minutes more. Blend cold water into cornstarch. Stir into soup. Pour egg slowly into hot soup in a thin stream, beating constantly with fork till egg cooks and shreds finely. Cook soup till slightly thickened and bubbly. Remove from heat. Stir in thinly sliced green onion. Makes 6 to 8 servings.

Pork-Shrimp Meatball Soup (pictured on page 2)

- 1 slightly beaten egg
- 2 tablespoons soy sauce
- 2 tablespoons fine dry bread crumbs
- 1 tablespoon finely chopped onion
- ¼ teaspoon ground ginger
- ½ pound ground pork
- 1 4½-ounce can shrimp, drained and finely chopped
- 1 medium onion, chopped
- 10 teaspoons instant chicken bouillon granules
  Few sprigs parsley
- 1 bay leaf
- ½ teaspoon dried rosemary, crushed
- 1½ cups shredded lettuce

In bowl thoroughly combine egg, soy sauce, bread crumbs, the 1 tablespoon onion, and ginger. Add pork and shrimp; mix well. Shape into 60 small meatballs, using about 1½ teaspoons mixture for each. In Dutch oven mix the remaining onion, bouillon granules, parsley, bay leaf, rosemary, 10 cups *water,* and ½ teaspoon *salt;* bring to boiling. Add meatballs; return to boiling. Cover; simmer 15 minutes. To serve, remove bay leaf and stir in lettuce. Makes 16 to 20 servings.

Crab and Spinach Soup

- 6 cups Homemade Chicken Broth (see recipe, page 54)
- ¼ cup finely chopped onion
- 2 tablespoons dry sherry
- 1 teaspoon grated gingerroot
- ½ teaspoon salt
- 4 cups small fresh spinach leaves
- 1 7½-ounce can crab meat, drained, flaked, and cartilage removed

In large saucepan or Dutch oven combine chicken broth, chopped onion, sherry, gingerroot, salt, and ⅛ teaspoon *pepper.* Bring to boiling. Add spinach leaves and crab. Return to boiling. Simmer, covered, 5 minutes. Makes 6 to 8 servings.

Savory Wonton Soup

1 beaten egg
¼ cup finely chopped onion
¼ cup finely chopped water chestnuts
1 tablespoon soy sauce
2 teaspoons grated gingerroot
½ teaspoon sugar
¼ teaspoon salt
⅛ teaspoon pepper
½ pound ground pork
1 4½-ounce can shrimp, drained and chopped
40 wonton skins *or* 10 egg roll skins, cut in quarters
6 cups Homemade Chicken Broth (see recipe, page 54)
1 cup thinly sliced Chinese cabbage
1 cup thinly sliced fresh mushrooms
1 6-ounce package frozen pea pods, thawed and halved lengthwise
½ cup thinly sliced bamboo shoots
4 green onions, bias-sliced into 1½-inch lengths

For wonton filling, in bowl combine egg, finely chopped onion, water chestnuts, soy sauce, gingerroot, sugar, salt, and pepper. Add ground pork and shrimp; mix well.

Position wonton skin with one point toward you. Spoon 1 rounded teaspoon of filling just off center of skin. Fold bottom point of wonton skin over the filling; tuck point under filling (see sketches on page 25). Roll once to cover filling, leaving about 1 inch at the top of skin that's not rolled. Moisten the right-hand corner of skin with water. Grasp the right- and left-hand corners of skin; bring these corners toward you below the filling. overlap the left-hand corner over the right-hand corner; press to seal. *(Use half the wontons for the soup. Wrap, label, and freeze remaining wontons for up to 1 month. Deep-fat fry thawed wontons as directed in recipe on page 25 or use them in another recipe of this soup.)*

In a large saucepan bring 8 cups *water* to boiling. Drop 20 wontons, one at a time, into boiling water. Simmer, uncovered, about 3 minutes. Remove from heat and rinse wontons with cold water; drain thoroughly. In same large saucepan bring chicken broth to boiling. Add Chinese cabbage, mushrooms, pea pods, bamboo shoots, and the wontons. Simmer, uncovered, 4 to 5 minutes. Stir in green onion. Ladle soup into individual serving bowls. Makes 6 to 8 servings.

Egg Drop Soup

2 13¾-ounce cans chicken broth
1 tablespoon cornstarch
1 well-beaten egg
2 tablespoons sliced green onion

In saucepan slowly stir the chicken broth into cornstarch. Cook, stirring constantly, till slightly thickened. Slowly pour in the well-beaten egg; stir once gently. Remove from heat. Garnish with green onion. Makes 4 servings.

Chicken Velvet and Corn Soup

1 whole small chicken breast, skinned, split, and boned
2¾ cups Homemade Chicken Broth (see recipe, page 54)
1½ teaspoons cornstarch
¼ teaspoon salt
⅛ teaspoon pepper
1 egg white
1 8-ounce can cream-style corn
2 tablespoons cold water
1 tablespoon cornstarch
½ teaspoon sesame oil (optional)
1 thin slice boiled ham, finely chopped

Place chicken breast pieces between two sheets of plastic wrap. Working out from center, pound chicken pieces to ¼-inch thickness. Remove plastic wrap. With sharp cleaver or knife, finely chop chicken. In mixer bowl combine chicken, ¼ *cup* chicken broth, the 1½ teaspoons cornstarch, salt, and pepper. Beat with electric mixer till well blended. With clean beaters, beat egg white till fluffy but not stiff; fold into chicken mixture. In large saucepan or Dutch oven, bring remaining 2½ cups chicken broth to boiling. Stir in cream-style corn. Slowly blend cold water into the 1 tablespoon cornstarch. Stir into broth along with sesame oil, if desired, and the chicken mixture. Cook and stir for 2 minutes. To serve, garnish with finely chopped boiled ham. Makes 3 or 4 servings.

Delicious and beautiful describe *Yosenabe* (see recipe, page 50), *Egg Drop Soup,* and *Savory Wonton Soup.*

Steaming Everything from Appetizers to Desserts

Serve *Steamed Pork and Vegetable Dumplings* or *Pork-Filled Buns* as appetizers and *Onion Rolls* as a bread (see recipes above and on page 60).

Steamed Pork and Vegetable Dumplings

2 cups all-purpose flour	1 green onion
⅔ cup boiling water	1 cup chopped cabbage
¼ cup cold water	1 tablespoon dry sherry
½ pound boneless pork	1 tablespoon soy sauce
	1½ teaspoons cornstarch
	½ teaspoon salt
	¼ teaspoon sugar

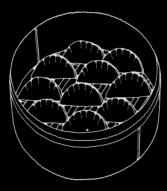

Fill dumpling; moisten edges of dough and pinch together to seal, as shown.

In mixing bowl combine flour and boiling water, stirring constantly with fork or chopsticks. Add cold water; mix with hands until dough forms ball (dough will be sticky). Cover; set aside.

With sharp cleaver or knife, finely chop the pork and green onion. Combine pork, green onion, and cabbage. Stir together sherry, soy sauce, cornstarch, salt, and sugar; add to meat mixture and mix with hands. Set aside.

Divide dough in half. Return half of dough to covered bowl. On well floured surface roll other half to about a 1/16-inch thickness. Cut with 2½-inch round cutter. Place about 1 teaspoonful of meat mixture in center of each dough circle. Lightly moisten edges of dough; bring dough up around filling and pinch together to seal, as shown. To position on greased steamer rack, flatten bottom so edge stands upright, as shown. Repeat with remaining dough and filling. Over high heat, bring water for steaming to boiling. Set steamer rack over boiling water. Cover steamer; steam about 15 minutes. Makes about 48.

Steaming hints: You'll get equally good results with a metal steamer, a bamboo steamer set over a wok or skillet, as shown, or a steamer substitute (see sketch). Just bring the water to boiling over high heat and make sure the water level is within 1½ inches of the steamer rack. Then, reduce heat to maintain a gentle boil and place food in steamer. Cover the steamer and steam till food is done. Add more boiling water if necessary, but avoid "peeking" as this lets steam escape.

Position dumplings on rack, flattening bottoms so edges stand upright.

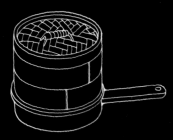

Position layers of bamboo steamer over boiling water in skillet or wok.

For steamer substitute, invert heat-proof bowl in Dutch oven. Add water and bring to boil. Then, set rack on bowl.

Pork-Filled Buns *(pictured on pages 58-59)*

3¼ to 3¾ cups all-purpose flour
 1 package active dry yeast
1¼ cups milk
 1 tablespoon sugar
 1 tablespoon cooking oil
 ½ teaspoon salt
 2 tablespoons finely chopped
    onion
 1 small clove garlic, minced
 1 tablespoon cooking oil
 ¾ cup finely chopped Oven
    Barbecued Pork (see recipe,
    page 75)
 ⅓ cup water
 2 tablespoons soy sauce
 2 teaspoons cornstarch
 2 teaspoons sugar
 ½ teaspoon grated gingerroot

In small mixer bowl combine *2 cups* of the flour and the yeast. In small saucepan heat milk just till warm (115-120°). Stir together warm milk, the 1 tablespoon sugar, 1 tablespoon oil, and salt. Add milk mixture to flour in bowl; beat at low speed of electric mixer for ½ minute, scraping sides of bowl constantly. Beat 3 minutes at high speed. By hand, stir in enough of the remaining flour to make a moderately soft dough. Knead on lightly floured surface till smooth and elastic (5 to 8 minutes). Shape into a ball. Place in lightly greased bowl, turning once to grease surface. Cover and let rise in warm place till double (45 to 60 minutes). Punch down; turn out on lightly floured surface. Shape into 10 balls. Cover; let rest 5 minutes.

Meanwhile, cook onion and garlic in 1 tablespoon hot oil till onion is tender but not brown. Add Oven Barbecued Pork; cook and stir till heated through. Stir water and soy sauce into cornstarch and the 2 teaspoons sugar; add to pork mixture. Cook and stir till thickened; remove from heat. On lightly floured surface, roll each ball of dough to a 3½-inch circle. Place a rounded tablespoon of pork mixture in center of each dough circle. Bring edges of dough up around filling, stretching a little till edges *just* meet; pinch to seal. Meanwhile, over high heat, bring water for steaming to boiling. Place buns, seam side down, on lightly greased steamer racks so sides don't touch; do not let rise. (If all buns won't fit on steamer rack, refrigerate part while others steam.) Place steamer rack over boiling water. Cover steamer; steam buns 15 to 17 minutes. Makes 10.

Onion Rolls *(pictured on pages 58-59)*

2¾ to 3¼ cups all-purpose flour
 1 package active dry yeast
 1 cup milk
 ¼ cup shortening
 1 teaspoon salt
 2 tablespoons butter *or*
    margarine, melted
 ½ cup thinly sliced green onion

In mixer bowl combine *1¼ cups* of the flour and the yeast. In saucepan heat together milk, shortening, and salt just till warm (115-120°), stirring constantly. Add to dry mixture in mixer bowl. Beat at low speed of electric mixer for ½ minute, scraping sides of bowl constantly. Beat 3 minutes at high speed. By hand, stir in enough of the remaining flour to make a moderately stiff dough. Turn out onto a lightly floured surface and knead till smooth and elastic (8 to 10 minutes). Shape into a ball. Place dough in lightly greased bowl; turn once to grease surface. Cover; let rise in warm place till double (about 1½ hours).

Punch dough down; turn out onto lightly floured surface. Divide dough in half. Cover; let rest for 10 minutes. Roll *half* the dough to a 10x6-inch rectangle. Brush with *half* melted butter or margarine; sprinkle with *half* green onion. Roll up jelly roll-style, starting with long side. Cut into 10 rolls. Using handle of fork, press each roll firmly across middle. Repeat with remaining dough, butter, and onion. Cover and let rise in warm place for 25 minutes. Meanwhile, over high heat, bring water for steaming to boiling. Place rolls on lightly greased steamer racks so sides don't touch. Set steamer racks over boiling water; cover. Steam rolls for 20 minutes. Makes 20.

Meat-Stuffed Eggplant *Korean*

1 large eggplant
2 slightly beaten eggs
½ teaspoon salt
⅛ teaspoon pepper
⅓ cup chopped onion
1 clove garlic, minced
1 tablespoon sesame seed, toasted
½ pound ground beef
¼ pound ground pork
8 green onions, thinly sliced
1 4-ounce can chopped
    mushrooms, drained
1 teaspoon instant beef bouillon
    granules
2 tablespoons soy sauce
1 tablespoon cornstarch

Halve eggplant lengthwise. Hollow out eggplant halves, leaving a ¾-inch shell. Chop ½ cup of the eggplant pulp and set aside; discard remaining pulp. In mixing bowl combine eggs, salt, and pepper. Add the ½ cup chopped eggplant, chopped onion, garlic, and sesame seed; add ground meats and mix thoroughly. Sprinkle eggplant shells generously with *salt*. Stuff with meat mixture.

Over high heat, bring water for steaming to boiling. Add *half* of the green onions to boiling water in steamer. Place stuffed eggplant on steamer rack over boiling water; cover and steam about 45 minutes or till meat is done.

Carefully remove stuffed eggplant and keep warm. Measure 1 cup of the water from steamer; pour into small saucepan. Stir in remaining green onions, the mushrooms, and bouillon granules. Blend soy sauce into cornstarch; stir into mushroom mixture. Cook and stir till thickened and bubbly. Serve over stuffed eggplant. Makes 4 servings.

Rice and Pork Balls with Pea Pods

1 slightly beaten egg
1 tablespoon soy sauce
1 teaspoon grated gingerroot
½ teaspoon salt
½ teaspoon sugar
1 pound lean ground pork
½ cup chopped fresh mushrooms
¼ cup finely chopped water
    chestnuts
1 tablespoon thinly sliced green
    onion
1½ cups cooked long grain rice
3 cups fresh pea pods *or* 2 6-ounce
    packages frozen pea pods,
    thawed
1 teaspoon butter *or* margarine
1 teaspoon soy sauce

Combine egg, the 1 tablespoon soy sauce, gingerroot, salt, and sugar. Add pork, mushrooms, water chestnuts, and green onion; mix thoroughly. Form meat mixture into 30 meatballs. Roll meatballs in cooked rice, pressing down gently, but firmly, so rice adheres to meat mixture. Over high heat, bring water for steaming to boiling. Place pork balls on one steamer rack; place rack over boiling water. Cover steamer; steam about 15 minutes. Add pea pods to a second rack of steamer; place atop first rack. Cover and continue steaming meatballs and pea pods 15 minutes more or till done (add more boiling water to steamer, if necessary). Toss pea pods with butter or margarine and the 1 teaspoon soy sauce; serve with meatballs. Makes 6 servings.

Make Full Use of Your Steamer

When you have a multi-layered bamboo or aluminum steamer, it's easy to serve an Oriental-style meal with several main dishes (see menu planning information on page 92). Simply put a separate dish on each layer of the steamer. Then, with the addition of another type of entrée that requires last-minute preparation, you can easily ready a full Oriental-style meal.

Also, take advantage of recipes such as Rice and Pork Balls with Pea Pods (see above) that steam the meat and vegetables on separate layers.

Steamed Savory Custard *Japanese*

2 **dried mushrooms**
½ **of a small chicken breast, skinned and boned (4 ounces)**
1 **tablespoon soy sauce**
1 **tablespoon dry sherry**
6 **spinach leaves, cut into 1½-inch pieces**
6 **small raw shrimp, shelled and deveined**
3 **slightly beaten eggs**
2½ **cups Homemade Chicken Broth (see recipe, page 54)** *or* **Dashi (see recipe, page 54)**
¼ **teaspoon salt**

Soak mushrooms in warm water for 30 minutes; squeeze to drain well. Discard stems; chop mushrooms. Cut chicken into thin strips. Combine chicken, soy sauce, and sherry.

Pour hot water over spinach to wilt; drain. Divide and arrange mushrooms, chicken, spinach, and shrimp in six 6-ounce custard cups or Chawan-Mushi cups. Combine eggs, chicken broth or dashi, and salt; carefully pour over shrimp in cups. Cover *each* cup with foil.

Over high heat, bring water for steaming to boiling. Position cups on steamer rack (or racks) over boiling water. Cover and steam about 20 minutes or till knife inserted just off-center comes out clean. Serve as first course. Makes 6 servings.

Alternate cooking method: Prepare mixture and put in cups as above. Cover each cup with foil; set on wire rack in Dutch oven or deep skillet. Pour hot water around cups to depth of 1 inch above rack; cover Dutch oven or skillet. Bring water to simmering. Reduce heat; cook about 20 minutes or till knife inserted just off-center comes out clean.

Sake-Steamed Fish with Mushrooms

1 **pound fresh** *or* **frozen flounder** *or* **sole fillets**
  Salt
  Pepper
4 **thin slices lemon**
1 **cup sliced fresh mushrooms**
½ **cup sake**
  Hot cooked rice

Thaw fish, if frozen. Arrange fish fillets in 9-inch pie plate (or another shallow heat-proof dish that is at least 1 inch smaller than steamer rack). Sprinkle fish generously with salt and pepper. Arrange lemon slices atop fish; sprinkle with mushrooms. Drizzle sake over all.

Over high heat, bring water for steaming to boiling. Place pie plate on steamer rack over boiling water. Cover steamer and steam 12 to 15 minutes or till fish flakes easily when tested with a fork. Serve with rice. Makes 4 servings.

A Handy Gadget When Steaming

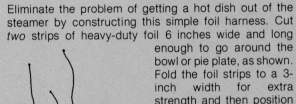

Eliminate the problem of getting a hot dish out of the steamer by constructing this simple foil harness. Cut *two* strips of heavy-duty foil 6 inches wide and long enough to go around the bowl or pie plate, as shown. Fold the foil strips to a 3-inch width for extra strength and then position them around the dish, as shown. Fold and crimp strips together at the top and grasp firmly. Carefully lower the dish into the steamer. Leave harness in place during steaming. To remove steamed food, grasp the harness (use pot holder) and lift the dish out.

Grand Old Man *(pictured on page 2)*

1 3-pound fresh *or* frozen drawn
   red snapper (with head and
   tail)
3 tablespoons snipped parsley
1 bay leaf
3 whole peppercorns
2 tablespoons butter *or* margarine
2 tablespoons all-purpose flour
   Dash white pepper
1 cup Homemade Chicken Broth
   (see recipe, page 54)
⅓ cup light cream
1 beaten egg yolk
1 green pepper, chopped
½ cup sliced green onion
1 teaspoon lemon juice
   Dash ground nutmeg
2 tablespoons grated gingerroot
2 tablespoons cooking oil

Thaw fish, if frozen. Pour water into fish poacher to depth of ½ inch. Add parsley, bay leaf, peppercorns, and 1 teaspoon *salt.* Bring to boiling. Place fish on greased rack; set into poacher. Cover; steam about 15 minutes or till fish flakes easily when tested with fork.

Meanwhile, melt butter or margarine in saucepan; blend in flour, white pepper, and ¼ teaspoon *salt.* Add chicken broth. Cook and stir till thickened; stir in cream. Gradually stir about ½ *cup* hot mixture into egg yolk; return to hot mixture. Add the green pepper and *half* the green onion. Cook over low heat, stirring constantly, till slightly thickened. Add lemon juice and nutmeg. Remove fish to warm platter; sprinkle remaining green onion and the gingerroot over fish. Heat oil; pour over all. Garnish fish with green onion brushes and parsley or Chinese parsley, if desired. Pass sauce. Makes 6 servings.

Fish with Black Bean Sauce

1 3-pound *or* 3 1-pound fresh *or*
   frozen whitefish *or* other fish
¼ cup fermented black beans
¼ cup sliced green onion
2 tablespoons finely slivered
   gingerroot
2 tablespoons cooking oil
2 cloves garlic, minced
⅛ teaspoon pepper
¼ cup sliced green onion
   Parsley

Thaw fish, if frozen. Sprinkle inside cavity of fish lightly with *salt.* Score fish several times on both sides, cutting about ¼ inch deep. Rinse fermented black beans. Combine black beans, ¼ cup green onion, gingerroot, cooking oil, garlic, and pepper. Spoon some of the bean mixture into cavity of fish and remaining mixture into slits. Pour water into fish poacher to ½-inch depth; bring to boiling. Place fish on greased rack; set into poacher. Cover; steam about 30 minutes for large fish (10 minutes for small fish) or till fish flakes easily when tested with fork. Garnish with ¼ cup green onion and parsley. Makes 6 servings.

Alternate Cooking Method: Halve large fish crosswise to fit in steamer. Position fish on greased steamer rack. Over high heat, bring water for steaming to boiling. Place steamer rack over boiling water. Cover; steam about 30 minutes for large fish (10 minutes for smaller fish) or till fish flakes easily when tested with fork. Garnish with sliced green onion and parsley to conceal the cut.

Steamed Oysters with Chicken *Korean*

2 whole chicken breasts, skinned,
   split, and boned
1 beaten egg
¼ cup pine nuts *or* almonds,
   chopped
2 tablespoons sliced green onion
1 small clove garlic, minced
1 tablespoon sesame seed, toasted
½ pint shucked oysters, drained

Chop chicken. Combine chicken, egg, pine nuts or almonds, green onion, garlic, sesame seed, ¾ teaspoon *salt,* and dash *pepper.* Turn chicken mixture into 9-inch pie plate (or another shallow heat-proof dish that is at least 1 inch smaller than steamer rack). Arrange oysters atop. Cover with foil. Over high heat, bring water for steaming to boiling. Place pie plate on steamer rack over boiling water. Cover and steam for 20 to 25 minutes or till done. Spoon off any excess liquid. Makes 4 to 6 servings.

Szechwan Pork-Stuffed Cucumbers

4 **large cucumbers**
 Salt
1 **egg**
½ **pound ground pork**
4 **green onions, sliced**
1 **small clove garlic, minced**
½ **teaspoon salt**
¼ **teaspoon ground ginger**
¼ **teaspoon pepper**

Peel cucumbers; halve *crosswise*. Slice small piece from end of each cucumber half so cucumbers will sit up. Scoop out seeds and center of each cucumber half, leaving ¼-inch shell. Sprinkle shell generously with salt and set aside.

In small mixing bowl beat egg with fork. Add pork, onions, garlic, the ½ teaspoon salt, ginger, and pepper; mix thoroughly. Stuff pork mixture into cucumber shells. Stand cucumbers, filled ends up, on steamer rack (if cucumbers won't stand on steamer rack, stand them in a heat-proof bowl that's at least 1 inch smaller than steamer rack).

Over high heat, bring water for steaming to boiling. Set steamer rack over boiling water (or, set bowl on steamer rack over boiling water). Cover steamer; steam about 25 minutes or till done. Makes 4 servings.

Rice-Coated Beef Balls

⅔ **cup short grain rice**
1 **slightly beaten egg**
1 **small clove garlic, minced**
1 **teaspoon salt**
½ **teaspoon ground ginger**
¼ **teaspoon pepper**
1 **pound lean ground beef**
½ **cup finely chopped onion**

Cover rice with water and set aside. In mixing bowl combine egg, garlic, salt, ginger, and pepper; add ground beef and onion and mix well. Shape meat mixture into 24 meatballs. Drain rice; roll meatballs in rice till coated.

Over high heat, bring water for steaming to boiling. Position meatballs on greased steamer rack leaving space between them. Place steamer rack over boiling water. Cover; steam about 20 minutes or till done. Makes 6 servings.

Steamed Pork Slices

1 **pound boneless pork**
3 **tablespoons soy sauce**
2 **tablespoons finely chopped onion**
1 **tablespoon dry sherry**
1 **teaspoon sugar**
¼ **teaspoon Homemade Five Spice Powder (see recipe, page 31)**

Partially freeze pork; slice thinly into bite-size strips. In heat-proof bowl that is at least 1 inch smaller than steamer rack, combine soy sauce, onion, sherry, sugar, and five spice powder. Add pork; stir to combine. Over high heat, bring water for steaming to boiling. Place uncovered bowl on steamer rack over boiling water. Cover steamer; steam 40 to 45 minutes or till pork is done, stirring once or twice. Serve with hot cooked rice, if desired. Makes 4 servings.

Pork- and Shrimp-Stuffed Mushrooms

¼ **pound ground pork**
1 **4½-ounce can shrimp, drained and chopped**
3 **green onions, thinly sliced**
1 **tablespoon soy sauce**
2 **teaspoons cornstarch**
1 **small clove garlic, minced**
36 **fresh mushrooms, each about 1 inch in diameter (12 ounces)**

In mixing bowl stir together ground pork, shrimp, and green onions. With hands, mix in soy sauce, cornstarch, and garlic. Remove stems from mushrooms and reserve for another use. Lightly salt insides of mushrooms. Stuff each mushroom cap with about a teaspoon of pork mixture. Arrange mushrooms on steamer rack. Over high heat, bring water for steaming to boiling. Set steamer rack over boiling water. Cover steamer; steam 30 to 35 minutes or till done. Makes 36 appetizers.

A layered steamer lets you cook *Szechwan Pork-Stuffed Cucumbers* and *Rice-Coated Beef Balls* at the same time.

Steamed Chicken with Chinese Sausage

4 dried mushrooms
¼ cup finely chopped onion
¼ cup dry sherry
1 teaspoon salt
2½ to 3 pounds chicken breasts
    and/or thighs, skinned
1 cup sliced Chinese sausage *or*
    cubed salami (about 5 ounces)

Soak mushrooms in warm water for 30 minutes; squeeze to drain well. Discard stems; chop mushrooms. Combine mushrooms, onion, sherry, and salt. Arrange chicken in shallow heat-proof dish or casserole that is at least 1 inch smaller than steamer rack. Top chicken with Chinese sausage or salami. Spoon mushroom mixture over.

Over high heat, bring water for steaming to boiling. Place uncovered dish on steamer rack; set rack over boiling water. Cover; steam for 40 to 45 minutes or till done, rearranging pieces once or twice to assure even cooking. Serve broth in bowls along with the chicken. Makes 4 servings.

Steamed Fish Steaks

2 large *or* 4 small fresh *or* frozen
    halibut *or* other fish steaks
4 dried mushrooms
4 green onions, bias-sliced into
    1-inch lengths
3 tablespoons soy sauce
2 tablespoons dry sherry
1½ teaspoons grated gingerroot

Thaw fish, if frozen. Soak dried mushrooms in warm water for 30 minutes; squeeze to drain well. Discard stems. Combine green onions, soy sauce, sherry, and gingerroot. Over high heat, bring water for steaming to boiling. Arrange fish steaks in heat-proof pan or dish that is at least 1 inch smaller than steamer rack. Do not overlap fish. Pour green onion mixture over fish steaks. Top fish steaks with dried mushrooms. Place uncovered pan or dish on steamer rack over boiling water. Cover and steam fish for 20 to 25 minutes or till fish flakes easily when tested with fork; drain. Makes 4 servings.

Keep Your Cleaver Sharp

Nothing will dampen your enthusiasm for Oriental cooking faster than trying to use a dull cleaver or knife. The Oriental technique of thinly slicing meat and vegetables demands a sharp blade. So, make it a habit to sharpen your cleaver and knives before each use.

For best results, sharpen cleaver and knives with a hand-held sharpening steel or stone. With the steel or stone in one hand, hold the cleaver or knife in the other hand at a 20° angle to the sharpener. Draw the blade edge over the sharpener, using a motion that goes across and down at the same time, as shown. Turn the blade over, reverse directions, and sharpen the other side the same number of times.

Steamed Chinese Cabbage

6 **dried mushrooms**
1 **medium head Chinese cabbage,**
    cut into 1½-inch-thick slices
½ **cup finely chopped, fully cooked**
    ham
1 **teaspoon instant chicken**
    bouillon granules
¼ **cup boiling water**

Soak mushrooms in warm water for 30 minutes; squeeze to drain well. Chop mushrooms, discarding stems. Place Chinese cabbage in a heat-proof bowl that is at least 1 inch smaller than steamer rack. Sprinkle mushrooms and ham over cabbage. Dissolve bouillon granules in boiling water; pour over cabbage. Over high heat, bring water for steaming to boiling. Place uncovered bowl on steamer rack over boiling water. Cover steamer; steam about 25 minutes, stirring gently once or twice. Drain before serving. Makes 6 to 8 servings.

Eight-Precious Pudding

8 **ounces pitted whole dates,**
    chopped (1⅓ cups)
¾ **cup water**
¼ **cup sugar**
½ **teaspoon vanilla**
3 **cups water**
1½ **cups short grain rice**
1 **teaspoon salt**
1 **teaspoon vanilla**
½ **cup sugar**
2 **tablespoons butter or margarine**
½ **cup chopped mixed candied**
    fruits and peels
10 **to 12 whole blanched almonds**
    Almond Glaze

In small saucepan combine dates, the ¾ cup water, and the ¼ cup sugar; bring to boiling. Cook over low heat, stirring constantly, about 4 minutes or till thick. Stir in the ½ teaspoon vanilla; set aside to cool.

In another saucepan combine the 3 cups water, rice, salt, and the 1 teaspoon vanilla. Bring to boil; reduce heat and cook, covered, for 15 minutes or till water is absorbed. Stir in the ½ cup sugar and butter or margarine.

Meanwhile, decoratively arrange mixed candied fruits and peels in bottom of buttered 1½-quart casserole or heat-proof bowl (make sure casserole or bowl is at least 1 inch smaller than steamer rack). Arrange almonds in ring around candied fruits and peels. Carefully spoon *half* of the rice mixture into casserole or bowl, being careful not to disturb fruit and nut design. Pat rice up around sides of casserole or bowl to form shell. Mix remaining rice with date mixture. Spoon into rice shell; pat surface even. Cover with foil.

Over high heat, bring water for steaming to boiling. Place casserole or bowl on steamer rack over boiling water. Cover and steam 45 to 60 minutes. Carefully unmold hot pudding. Serve pudding warm with Almond Glaze. Makes 10 to 12 servings.

Almond Glaze: In small saucepan combine ¼ cup *sugar* and 1 tablespoon *cornstarch*. Stir in 1 cup cold *water*. Cook and stir till thickened and bubbly. Remove from heat; stir in 1 tablespoon *butter and* ¼ teaspoon *almond extract*.

Steamed Sponge Cake

4 **egg yolks**
2 **tablespoons water**
½ **cup sugar**
½ **teaspoon vanilla**
¼ **teaspoon lemon extract**
4 **egg whites**
½ **cup sugar**
1 **cup all-purpose flour**
1 **teaspoon baking powder**
¼ **teaspoon salt**

Over high heat, bring water for steaming to boiling. In small mixer bowl beat egg yolks till thick and lemon-colored (4 minutes); beat in the 2 tablespoons water. Gradually beat in ½ cup sugar; beat in vanilla and lemon extract. Wash beaters well. In large mixer bowl beat egg whites till soft peaks form; gradually add ½ cup sugar, beating constantly till stiff peaks form. Fold yolks into whites. Stir together flour, baking powder, and salt; fold into egg mixture. Turn batter into greased and floured 8x8x2-inch baking pan.

Place uncovered pan on steamer rack over boiling water. Cover steamer with dish towel; cover with steamer lid. Steam about 25 minutes or till done. Serve warm. Serves 9.

Grilling and Roasting Meats

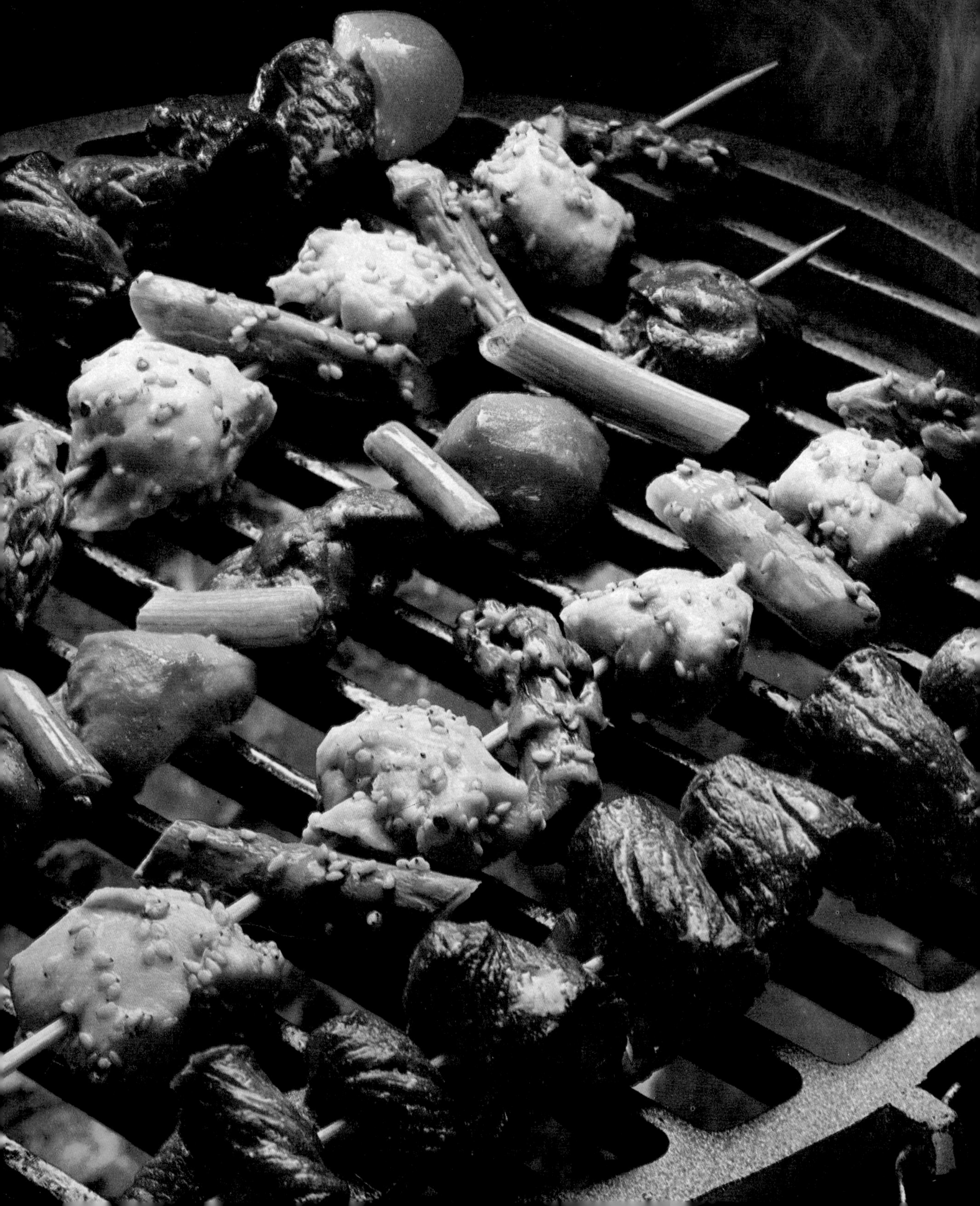

Beef Teriyaki *Japanese*

1½ pounds boneless beef
    tenderloin *or* sirloin,
    cut 1 inch thick
4 cloves garlic

½ cup soy sauce
¼ cup sake *or* dry sherry
2 tablespoons sugar
2 teaspoons dry mustard
   Preserved kumquats
   (optional)

Partially freeze beef; thinly slice across grain into bite-size strips. To peel garlic easily, smash with cleaver as shown; peel garlic and mince. Combine garlic, soy sauce, sake or sherry, sugar, and mustard. Add meat to soy mixture and let stand 15 minutes at room temperature. Drain meat, reserving marinade. Thread meat strips accordion-style on small skewers as shown. If desired, halve kumquats and add a kumquat half to end of each skewer. For skewered foods, line up *hot* coals in parallel rows in the firebox and around the edge of grill. Arrange skewers on the grate directly above spaces between briquette rows so meat fat will not drip on coals (see sketch). Grill skewers over *hot* coals 5 to 7 minutes or till desired doneness. Turn and baste with marinade frequently. Makes 18 appetizers.

Grilling hints: To start charcoal, pile briquettes into a pyramid or mound in center of the firebox as shown. Drizzle liquid lighter or jelly fire starter over the whole surface of charcoal. Wait 1 minute, then ignite with a match. Let the coals burn 20 to 30 minutes or till they die down to a glow and no areas of black show (the coals should look ash-gray by day and glow red after dark). When coals are ready, use a fire rake or long-handled tongs to spread coals in a single layer. Hold your hand, palm-side down, just above coals at the height the food will be cooking. Begin counting "one thousand one, one thousand two, etc." If you need to withdraw your hand after two seconds, the coals are hot.

Japanese and Korean grilled specialties include *Beef Teriyaki, Chicken-Asparagus Skewers,* and *Yakitori* (see recipes above and on page 74).

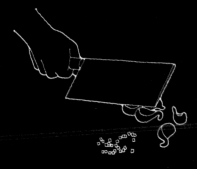

To peel garlic easily, first smash it with the flat side of a cleaver or large knife.

Thread meat strips accordion-style on bamboo or metal skewers as shown to assure even cooking.

To start charcoal, first pile the briquettes in pyramid in center of the hibachi or grill. Add lighter; ignite.

When grilling skewered foods, arrange hot coals in parallel rows and position skewers above spaces between coals.

Skewered Beef and Onion

6 green onions
¼ cup soy sauce
1 tablespoon cooking oil
1 tablespoon lemon juice
2 teaspoons sugar
1 pound beef sirloin steak, cut in 1-inch pieces

Cut onions in 1½-inch-long pieces. Mix soy sauce, oil, lemon juice, sugar, 2 tablespoons *water,* and ¼ teaspoon *pepper.* Marinate beef and onion in soy mixture 30 minutes; drain. Reserve marinade. On bamboo skewers alternately thread beef and onion pieces. Grill over *hot* coals till meat is desired doneness (allow 12 to 15 minutes for medium). Turn often; brush occasionally with reserved marinade. Serves 4.

Grilled Marinated Beef *Korean*

1½ pounds beef sirloin steak, cut ½ inch thick
¼ cup soy sauce
2 green onions, finely chopped
2 cloves garlic, minced
2 tablespoons sugar
2 tablespoons sesame oil
2 tablespoons dry sherry
⅛ teaspoon pepper

Cut meat into serving-size pieces; score on both sides. Place meat in shallow pan. Mix soy sauce, onions, garlic, sugar, oil, sherry, and pepper. Pour over beef and let stand 1 hour at room temperature; turn once. Drain. Place meat over *medium* coals. (Hold hand, palm-side down, just above coals. Count "one thousand one, one thousand two, etc." If you need to withdraw your hand after four seconds, the coals are medium.) Grill till desired doneness (allow about 15 minutes for medium). Garnish with additional green onion, if desired. Makes 4 to 6 servings.

Barbecued Short Ribs *Korean*

3 pounds beef plate short ribs, cut in serving-size pieces
¾ cup soy sauce
2 green onions
1 clove garlic, minced
1 teaspoon instant beef bouillon granules
2 tablespoons sesame oil
1 tablespoon sugar
1 tablespoon vinegar
1 teaspoon sesame seed, toasted
½ teaspoon dry mustard

Trim excess fat from short ribs. In large Dutch oven mix ½ *cup* soy sauce, onions, garlic, beef bouillon granules, and ½ cup *water.* Add rib pieces. Cover; simmer 1½ hours or till tender. Drain. Mix remaining soy sauce, sesame oil, sugar, vinegar, sesame seed, dry mustard, and ⅛ teaspoon *pepper.* Place ribs over *slow* coals. (Hold hand, palm-side down, just above coals. Count "one thousand one, one thousand two, etc." If you need to withdraw your hand after five or six seconds, the coals are slow.) Grill 20 to 30 minutes; turn and brush frequently with the soy sauce-sesame mixture. Serves 6.

Teriyaki Appetizer Ribs

4 pounds meaty pork spareribs, sawed in half across bones
½ cup soy sauce
2 tablespoons cooking oil
2 tablespoons lemon juice
1 tablespoon brown sugar
2 cloves garlic, minced
1 teaspoon ground ginger
¼ teaspoon pepper
2 tablespoons honey

Cut meat in 2-rib portions. Mix soy, oil, lemon juice, brown sugar, garlic, ginger, and pepper. Place ribs in shallow pan; pour soy mixture over. Cover; marinate in refrigerator 4 to 6 hours or overnight. Occasionally spoon marinade over. Remove ribs, reserving marinade. Place ribs over *slow* coals, bone side down. (Hold hand, palm-side down, just above coals. Count "one thousand one, one thousand two, etc." If you need to withdraw your hand after five or six seconds, coals are slow.) Grill about 25 minutes (add less meaty ribs after about 10 minutes). Turn ribs, meaty side down; grill 15 to 20 minutes more. Stir honey into reserved marinade; brush often over ribs during last 5 minutes. Makes about 26.

Bean-Sauced Spareribs

3 to 4 pounds pork spareribs
½ cup sweet bean sauce
2 tablespoons water
2 tablespoons dry sherry
2 tablespoons soy sauce
2 cloves garlic, minced

Cut ribs into 2-rib portions. In large covered saucepan or Dutch oven cook ribs in enough boiling salted water to cover for 45 to 60 minutes or till ribs are just tender. Drain well. Combine sweet bean sauce, the 2 tablespoons water, dry sherry, soy sauce, and garlic. Brush ribs with bean sauce mixture. Place ribs over *slow* coals. (Hold hand, palm-side down, just above coals. Count "one thousand one, one thousand two, etc." If you need to withdraw your hand after five or six seconds, the coals are slow.) Grill about 45 minutes or till done; turn ribs occasionally, brushing with bean sauce mixture. Makes 3 or 4 servings.

Skewered Pork and Carrots

4 medium carrots, bias-sliced into ½-inch lengths
1 pound boneless pork, cut in 1-inch pieces
¼ cup dry sherry
2 tablespoons sesame oil
1 tablespoon sesame seed, toasted and crushed
1 teaspoon salt
1 teaspoon grated onion
1 small clove garlic, minced
⅛ teaspoon pepper

In covered saucepan cook carrots in a small amount of boiling salted water for 5 to 7 minutes or till just tender; drain well. Place carrots and pork in plastic bag. Combine sherry, sesame oil, sesame seed, salt, onion, garlic, and pepper. Pour sherry mixture over carrots and pork. Close bag. Marinate in the refrigerator at least 4 hours. Drain carrots and pork, reserving marinade. Thread carrot and pork pieces alternately on skewers. Place over *medium* coals. (Hold hand, palm-side down, just above the coals. Count "one thousand one, one thousand two, etc. If you need to withdraw your hand after four seconds, the coals are medium.) Grill about 15 minutes or till done; turn skewers and brush with reserved marinade frequently. Makes 4 servings.

Tips for Charcoal Grilling

• If a charcoal fire is too hot, try one of these techniques: raise the grill grate, lower the firebox, close the air vents, or remove some of the hot coals.

• To make a charcoal fire hotter, tap the ashes off the burning coals with tongs, move the briquettes closer together, lower the grate, raise the firebox, or open the air vents to allow more air to move through the grill.

• Control fire flare-ups caused by meat fat dripping on the coals by spacing the briquettes farther apart or removing a few coals to reduce the heat. Always keep a pump-spray bottle filled with water nearby to use to sprinkle water over flare-ups. Be careful not to soak the coals or the fire will go out.

• Save money by reusing charcoal. For a covered grill, simply lower the hood and close the air vents. When the coals are cool, they will be ready to use again. Or if you own an open unit, use tongs to transfer hot coals to a metal pail half full of water. When the coals are cool, drain and spread them on newspapers. Be sure to dry the charcoal completely or it will not relight.

Grilled Lamb, Mongolian-Style

2 pounds boneless lamb
½ cup water
⅓ cup soy sauce
3 tablespoons dry sherry
2 tablespoons thinly sliced green onion
3 whole black peppercorns, crushed
1 star anise *or* ½ teaspoon aniseed
1 clove garlic, minced
1 pound fresh spinach
12 green onions, cut in 2-inch lengths

Partially freeze lamb; thinly slice into bite-size strips. Place lamb in plastic bag. Combine water, soy sauce, sherry, thinly sliced green onion, crushed peppercorns, anise or aniseed, and garlic; pour over lamb. Close bag. Marinate 1 to 2 hours in refrigerator.

To make a foil pan to set atop grill, tear off a piece of 18-inch-wide heavy-duty foil twice the length of grill. Fold in half crosswise for a double thickness. Turn up all edges of foil 1½ inches. Miter corners securely and fold tips of corners toward inside for added strength. Lightly grease pan. Position on grill over *hot* coals.

Drain lamb. Discard marinade. Place enough lamb, spinach, and green onion pieces on foil pan to fill pan in a single layer; grill about 10 minutes or till desired doneness, turning occasionally. Repeat with remaining lamb, spinach, and onion pieces. Makes 6 servings.

Bacon-Wrapped Shrimp Appetizers

¼ cup soy sauce
1 tablespoon sugar
1 small clove garlic, minced
1 teaspoon grated gingerroot
1 pound fresh *or* frozen large shrimp
7 to 8 slices bacon

Combine soy sauce, sugar, garlic, gingerroot, and dash *pepper*; let stand 1 hour at room temperature. Thaw shrimp, if frozen. Shell and devein shrimp (see sketch on page 43). Cut bacon slices in thirds. Wrap a piece of bacon around each shrimp; skewer to secure. Grill bacon-wrapped shrimp over *hot* coals about 15 minutes or till done, turning and brushing with soy mixture frequently. Makes about 21 appetizers.

Grilled Fish Fillets

1½ pounds fresh *or* frozen fish fillets
¼ cup soy sauce
¼ cup dry sherry
¼ cup sesame seed, toasted and crushed
2 tablespoons cooking oil
2 teaspoons grated gingerroot

Thaw fish, if frozen. Combine soy sauce, sherry, sesame seed, oil, and gingerroot. Arrange fish in single layer in shallow dish; pour soy sauce mixture over fish. Marinate fish for 15 minutes at room temperature, turning fish once. Drain, reserving marinade. Place fish in well-greased wire grill basket. Grill over *hot* coals for 8 minutes. Turn fish and brush with marinade. Grill 7 to 9 minutes more or till fish flakes easily when tested with a fork. Makes 4 servings.

Soy-Marinated Perch Fillets

2 pounds fresh *or* frozen perch fillets
⅓ cup cooking oil
3 tablespoons soy sauce
2 tablespoons vinegar
2 tablespoons finely chopped onion

Thaw fish, if frozen. Mix oil, soy sauce, vinegar, and onion. Arrange fish in single layer in shallow dish; pour soy sauce mixture over. Marinate fish for 30 to 60 minutes at room temperature; turn occasionally. Drain, reserving marinade. Place fish in a well-greased wire grill basket. Grill over *hot* coals for 8 to 9 minutes. Turn fish and brush with marinade. Grill 6 to 8 minutes more or till fish flakes easily when tested with a fork. Makes 6 servings.

Plan a party around *Grilled Lamb, Mongolian-Style*. Guests can grill their own servings of lamb and vegetables.

Yakitori *Japanese* *(pictured on page 68)*

½ **cup soy sauce**
¼ **cup water**
¼ **cup sake *or* dry sherry**
1 **tablespoon sugar**
1 **teaspoon grated gingerroot**
½ **pound chicken livers, cut in half**
1 **whole large chicken breast, skinned, split, boned, and cut in 1-inch pieces**
6 **green onions, bias-sliced into 1-inch lengths**

In saucepan combine soy sauce, water, sake or sherry, sugar, and gingerroot. Boil 1 minute; cool. Marinate chicken livers, chicken cubes, and onion in soy mixture for 15 to 30 minutes at room temperature; turn once. Drain, reserving marinade. On skewers alternately thread chicken cubes, onion pieces, and chicken liver pieces. Grill over *hot* coals 8 to 10 minutes or till done; turn and brush occasionally with reserved marinade. Serves 4 or 5.

Chicken-Asparagus Skewers *Korean* *(pictured on page 68)*

¼ **pound fresh asparagus, cut into 1½-inch pieces**
2 **whole large chicken breasts, skinned, split, boned, and cut into 1-inch pieces**
1 **tablespoon sesame oil**
1 **tablespoon sesame seed, toasted**
1 **clove garlic, minced**
½ **teaspoon salt**
   Dash pepper
   Cooking oil

In covered saucepan cook asparagus in a small amount of boiling salted water for 5 minutes; drain. In bowl combine asparagus, chicken, sesame oil, sesame seed, garlic, salt, and pepper; mix well. Let stand 15 minutes. Thread asparagus and chicken pieces alternately on skewers. Brush asparagus with cooking oil. Place skewers over *medium* coals. (Hold hand, palm-side down, just above coals. Count "one thousand one, one thousand two, etc." If you need to withdraw your hand after four counts, the coals are *medium*.) Grill for 15 minutes or till done, brushing asparagus with oil once while grilling. Makes 4 servings.

Kowloon Duckling

   Hickory chips
1 **4- to 5-pound domestic duckling**
6 **to 8 green onions, cut up**
6 **sprigs parsley**
1 **clove garlic, minced**
½ **cup soy sauce**
2 **tablespoons honey**
2 **tablespoons lemon juice**
   Plum-Orange Sauce

About 1 hour before cooking, soak the hickory chips in enough water to cover. Drain chips. Stuff cavity of duckling with onions, parsley, and garlic. Skewer neck and body cavities closed; tie legs to tail securely with cord. In saucepan combine soy sauce, honey, and lemon juice; bring to boil. In *covered grill* arrange *slow* coals around edge of grill. (Hold hand, palm-side down, just above coals. Count "one thousand one, one thousand two, etc." If you need to withdraw your hand after five or six counts, the coals are *slow*.) Sprinkle coals with some of the dampened chips. Center heavy foil pan on grill, not directly over coals. Place duck, breast-side up, in foil pan. Lower grill hood. Grill for 2¼ to 2½ hours or till done. Sprinkle chips over coals every 30 minutes. Brush duck often with soy mixture. Remove drippings from pan as necessary. Serve with Plum-Orange Sauce. Makes 2 or 3 servings.

   Plum-Orange Sauce: Drain one 16-ounce can whole, un-pitted *purple plums,* reserving ¼ cup syrup. Force plums through a sieve, removing pits. In saucepan combine the sieved plums, reserved plum syrup, ¼ teaspoon grated *orange peel,* 3 tablespoons *orange juice,* 2 tablespoons *sugar,* ½ teaspoon *worcestershire sauce,* and ¼ teaspoon ground *cinnamon.* Bring to boil; reduce heat and simmer 10 minutes.

Oven Barbecued Pork

2 **pounds boneless pork loin**
¼ **cup soy sauce**
¼ **cup honey**
2 **tablespoons thinly sliced green**
    onion
2 **tablespoons dry sherry**
½ **teaspoon Homemade Five Spice**
    Powder (see recipe, page 31)

Cut pork crosswise into 1-inch-thick slices; place in a single layer in shallow dish. Mix soy sauce, honey, onion, sherry, and five spice powder. Pour over pork. Cover; marinate several hours or overnight in refrigerator, turning once or twice. Drain, reserving marinade. Place pork slices on rack in broiler pan. Bake in a 350° oven 50 to 60 minutes or till done; turn and brush occasionally with reserved marinade. Cut meat slices into thin strips. Serve separately or use as an ingredient in Pork-Filled Buns or Chicken and Pork Chow Mein (see index for recipe pages). Serves 8.

Sweet-Sour Glazed Riblets *(pictured on page 2)*

2½ **pounds pork spareribs, sawed in**
    half across bones
1 **13¼-ounce can pineapple**
    chunks
2 **tablespoons brown sugar**
1 **tablespoon cornstarch**
⅛ **teaspoon salt**
½ **cup cold water**
2 **tablespoons vinegar**
1 **tablespoon soy sauce**
1 **small green pepper, cut in 1-inch**
    pieces

Cut meat into 2-rib portions; season with salt and pepper. Place ribs, meaty side down, in large shallow roasting pan. Bake in 450° oven for 30 minutes. Drain off fat. Turn meaty side up. Reduce heat to 350°; bake 30 minutes more. Meanwhile, drain pineapple, reserving ⅓ cup syrup. In saucepan combine brown sugar, cornstarch, and salt. Blend in the reserved syrup, cold water, vinegar, and soy sauce. Cook and stir till thickened and bubbly. Stir in green pepper and pineapple. Cover; cook 5 minutes. Drain fat from ribs. Spoon sauce atop ribs. Bake 15 minutes more. Serves 8.

Peking Duck

One of the most flavorful, unique, and difficult to prepare dishes in the Oriental cuisine is Peking duck. Because it requires an expertly trained chef, special air-pumping equipment, and a kiln-type oven, Peking duck has become the domain of a select group of restaurants that pride themselves on their art, and is seldom prepared at home. The recipe begins with a specially bred Imperial Peking duckling that has been slaughtered and dressed with its head and neck intact. Air is forced (by means of mechanical pumps) through a small hole in the bird's neck to inflate the space between the skin and the meat. The bird is then tied or sewn together at both ends to retain the air. A malt-sugar or honey syrup is brushed all over the skin, and the bird is hung in the open air to dry for 24 hours. The final step is to roast the duckling, vertically, in a cylindrical oven till golden brown.

When Peking duck is served, the crispy skin is the most prized portion. It is cut in small pieces and arranged on a platter. Diners place a piece of skin on a thin wheat pancake, dip a green onion in hoisin sauce, and then roll everything up in the pancake. The duck meat is not as prized and can be served later in the meal or saved for another occasion.

Honey and Spice Duckling

2 teaspoons salt
2 teaspoons whole black pepper
  or Szechwan pepper,
  coarsely ground
1 teaspoon ground ginger
½ teaspoon Homemade Five Spice
  Powder (see recipe, page 31)
1 4- to 5-pound domestic duckling
¼ cup honey
2 tablespoons soy sauce

Combine salt, pepper, ginger, and five spice powder. Sprinkle cavity of duck with some of the salt mixture; rub remaining on skin. Skewer neck skin to back; tie legs to tail. Twist wing tips under back. Prick skin all over with fork. Place duckling, breast-side up, on rack in shallow roasting pan. Roast in a 375° oven for 1¾ to 2 hours, spooning off fat occasionally. Mix honey and soy sauce; baste duckling with soy mixture. Roast 15 to 20 minutes more or till drumstick moves easily in socket, basting often with soy mixture. Cut duckling Oriental-style (see tip, below). Serves 3 or 4.

Soy-Glazed Chicken

½ cup soy sauce
2 tablespoons finely chopped
  onion
2 cloves garlic, minced
1 tablespoon cooking oil
1 teaspoon Homemade Five Spice
  Powder (see recipe, page 31)
1 4- to 5-pound whole roasting
  chicken

Combine soy sauce, onion, garlic, cooking oil, five spice powder, 1½ teaspoons *salt,* and ¼ teaspoon *pepper.* Place chicken in plastic bag; set in a bowl. Pour soy sauce mixture over chicken; close bag. Refrigerate for 2 to 3 hours, turning chicken occasionally. Drain. Skewer neck skin to back. Tie legs securely to tail; twist wing tips under back. Place chicken, breast-side up, on rack in a shallow roasting pan. Roast in 375° oven about 1½ hours or till drumstick moves easily in socket. Makes 3 or 4 servings.

Cutting Roast Poultry Oriental-Style

To serve roast poultry with an Oriental flare, just follow these easy step-by-step cutting directions.
1. First, with the poultry breast-side up, cut in half lengthwise through the breast with a cleaver, as shown. Kitchen shears may help in finishing the cutting.
2. Cut off the wings and legs close to the body; set aside.
3. Cut off the backbone on each half of the bird. Then cut each part of the backbone into bite-size pieces and reassemble on a serving platter.
4. Cut each reserved wing and leg into two or three pieces and arrange on each side of the backbone.
5. Chop the remaining bird into bite-size pieces. Reassemble each half into its original shape as shown.

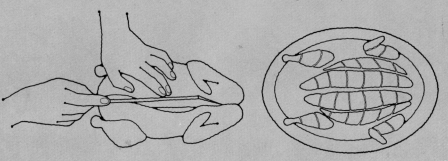

For Chinese cooking at its best, serve *Honey and Spice Duckling* cut into bite-size pieces Oriental-style (see tip).

Salads & Vegetables

All types of vegetables are used extensively in Oriental main dishes. However, there are relatively few all-vegetable dishes in the Oriental cuisine. The collection of recipes given here are representative of Chinese and Japanese salads and vegetables (you'll find several stir-fried vegetables on pages 20 to 23).

Don't reserve the intriguing bok choy, Chinese cabbage, bean sprouts, and pea pods only for Oriental dishes. Use any of them to dress up your favorite tossed salads. Try bean sprouts in casseroles and sandwiches. And remember buttered pea pods any time you need a simple vegetable dish (cook pea pods briefly in boiling salted water, drain, and add butter).

Fresh Bean Sprout-Cucumber Salad *(pictured above)*

2 cups fresh bean sprouts
2 medium cucumbers
¼ cup soy sauce
2 tablespoons vinegar
1 tablespoon sesame oil
1 teaspoon sugar
⅛ teaspoon dry mustard
Several dashes bottled hot pepper sauce
1 tablespoon sesame seed, toasted

Cook bean sprouts in boiling salted water for 2 minutes; drain. Chill bean sprouts. To score unpeeled cucumbers, run tines of fork down sides; thinly slice cucumbers. Arrange sliced cucumbers and bean sprouts on serving plate. In small screw-top jar combine soy sauce, vinegar, sesame oil, sugar, dry mustard, and bottled hot pepper sauce; cover and shake to mix well. Drizzle soy mixture over vegetables. Sprinkle with toasted sesame seed. Makes 6 to 8 servings.

Creamed Bok Choy

½ cup water
1 tablespoon soy sauce
½ teaspoon instant chicken bouillon granules
Several dashes pepper
Dash garlic powder
6 cups chopped bok choy
¼ cup light cream *or* milk
4 teaspoons cornstarch

In large saucepan combine water, soy sauce, bouillon granules, pepper, and garlic powder. Bring to boiling. Add bok choy. Reduce heat; cover and simmer about 5 minutes or till crisp-tender. Blend light cream or milk into cornstarch; stir into bok choy. Cook and stir till thickened and bubbly. Makes 6 servings.

Braised Chinese Vegetables

  6 **dried mushrooms**
 ¼ **cup dried lily buds**
  2 **tablespoons cooking oil**
  2 **cups chopped bok choy**
1½ **cups fresh pea pods** *or* **1 6-ounce**
      package frozen pea pods,
      thawed
  1 **cup fresh bean sprouts**
 ½ **cup sliced water chestnuts**
 ½ **cup Homemade Chicken Broth**
      (see recipe, page 54)
  2 **tablespoons soy sauce**
 ½ **teaspoon sugar**
  2 **tablespons dry sherry**
  2 **teaspoons cornstarch**

Soak dried mushrooms and lily buds in enough warm water to cover for 30 minutes; squeeze to drain well. Chop mushrooms, discarding stems. Cut lily buds into thirds. Preheat wok or large skillet over high heat; add oil. Stir-fry bok choy, pea pods, bean sprouts, and water chestnuts in hot oil for 2 minutes. Add mushrooms, lily buds, chicken broth, soy sauce, and sugar. Cover and cook 5 minutes. Blend dry sherry into cornstarch. Stir into vegetable mixture. Cook and stir till thickened and bubbly. Serve at once. Serves 6.

Fresh Broccoli Salad

1 **pound fresh broccoli**
2 **tablespoons vinegar**
1 **tablespoon soy sauce**
1 **tablespoon sesame oil**
1 **teaspoon sugar**
1 **tablespoon sesame seed, toasted**

Cut broccoli stalks lengthwise into uniform spears, following branching lines. Halve spears crosswise. Cook in 1 inch of boiling salted water for 10 to 15 minutes or till just done. Drain; chill broccoli. In screw-top jar combine vinegar, soy sauce, sesame oil, and sugar; cover and shake to mix well. Drizzle vinegar mixture over broccoli; toss gently. Sprinkle with toasted sesame seed. Makes 4 to 6 servings.

Homegrown Bean Sprouts

It's fun and easy to grow your own bean sprouts. Buy mung beans that have not been chemically treated, such as from a health food store or Oriental market. Carefully sort through the beans, selecting ⅓ cup of clean, whole beans. Wash them thoroughly. Place the beans in a bowl and cover them with lukewarm water, allowing enough water for beans to swell (they will almost double in size). Let stand overnight. Drain; rinse.

Wash three 1-quart jars; place about ¼ cup of the soaked beans in each jar. Cover tops of the jars with two layers of cheesecloth or nylon netting as shown; fasten each with two rubber bands or a screw-type canning lid band. Place the jars on their sides in a warm, dark place (68° to 75° F.). Once a day rinse the sprouts by pouring lukewarm water into the jars, swirling to moisten all the beans, then pouring off the water. In three or four days, the beans should sprout. Use the bean sprouts when they are 1½ to 2½ inches long.

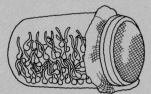

Noodles

Many varieties of
wheat flour noodles
as well as noodle-like
bean threads and rice
sticks are available at Oriental stores.
These noodles resemble common egg noodles except for their length. In
the following recipes, use either Oriental wheat flour noodles or egg noodles (bean threads and rice sticks don't have a common substitution).

When planning Oriental menus, include Fried Rice Sticks with Pork as
one of the main dishes. Or, as a change from rice, serve one of the following noodle dishes as a main dish accompaniment.

Soft-Fried Noodles with Vegetables (pictured above)

  4 **dried mushrooms**
  3 **cups fine noodles (6 ounces)**
 ⅓ **cup Homemade Chicken Broth**
      (see recipe, page 54)
  3 **tablespoons soy sauce**
  1 **teaspoon cornstarch**
  3 **tablespoons cooking oil**
  1 **cup coarsely shredded zucchini**
 ½ **cup fresh *or* canned bean**
      sprouts, drained
 ½ **cup coarsely shredded carrot**
 ½ **cup sliced green onion**
  1 **teaspoon grated gingerroot**

Soak dried mushrooms in enough warm water to cover for 30
minutes; squeeze to drain well. Chop mushrooms, discarding
stems.

Cook noodles according to package directions. Rinse in
cold water. Drain well. Blend chicken broth and soy sauce
into cornstarch; set aside.

Preheat wok or large skillet over high heat; add *1 tablespoon* of the cooking oil. Add *half* of the noodles; stir-fry for 5
to 7 minutes or till just beginning to brown. Remove to warm
plate. Repeat with another tablespoon oil and remaining
noodles; remove. Add remaining oil to *hot* wok or skillet. Add
mushrooms, zucchini, fresh or canned bean sprouts, carrot,
green onion, and gingerroot to wok or skillet; stir-fry 1 minute.
Stir chicken broth mixture and stir into vegetable mixture.
Cook and stir till thickened and bubbly. Stir in noodles; cover
and heat through. Serve warm with the desired main dish.
Makes 6 servings.

Chilled Noodles *Japanese*

1½ **cups fine noodles (3 ounces)**
 ¼ **cup thinly sliced green onion**
 ¼ **cup Dashi, chilled (see recipe,**
      page 54)
  2 **tablespoons soy sauce**
  1 **tablespoon dry sherry**
 ½ **teaspoon grated gingerroot**

Cook noodles according to package directions; drain well.
Cover with *ice water*; let stand till noodles are chilled. Drain
well. Combine noodles and green onion; set aside. Combine
dashi, soy sauce, dry sherry, and gingerroot. Serve noodles
with dashi mixture (each person drizzles as much dashi mixture on noodles as desired). Makes 3 or 4 servings.

Fried Rice Sticks with Pork

¼ **pound boneless pork**
Boiling water
4 **ounces dried rice sticks**
2 **tablespoons cooking oil**
1 **small clove garlic, minced**
⅓ **cup sliced green onion**
1 **cup fresh pea pods, halved**
lengthwise
1 **4-ounce can chopped**
mushrooms, drained
¼ **cup Homemade Chicken Broth**
(see recipe, page 54)
3 **tablespoons soy sauce**

Partially freeze pork; thinly slice pork and then cut into shreds. Pour enough boiling water over rice sticks to cover; let stand 5 minutes. Drain; rinse in cold water. Drain well.

Preheat wok or large skillet over high heat; add oil. Stir-fry garlic in hot oil for 30 seconds. Add pork and green onion; stir-fry 2 minutes. Remove pork and green onion. Add drained rice sticks; stir-fry 3 minutes. Stir in pork and green onion, pea pods, mushrooms, and chicken broth. Cover and cook 2 minutes. Stir in soy sauce. Cook, stirring constantly, 2 minutes more. Makes 3 or 4 servings.

Crusty Noodle Cakes

6 **cups water**
2 **tablespoons instant chicken**
bouillon granules
2 **cups medium noodles**
Cooking oil

In large saucepan or Dutch oven combine water and chicken bouillon granules; bring to boiling. Add noodles; boil for 8 to 10 minutes or till tender. Drain well. Divide noodles into four portions. With hands, shape and press each portion into a 3-inch patty. Let dry about 30 minutes. Pour cooking oil into wok or skillet to depth of ½ inch; heat oil. Fry noodle patties in hot oil for 3 to 4 minutes or till golden and crusty, turning once. Drain on paper toweling. Serve warm with desired main dish. Makes 4 servings.

Triple-Cooked Noodles

3 **cups medium noodles (4 ounces)**
Cooking oil for deep-fat frying
8 **cups water**
1 **teaspoon salt**

Cook noodles according to package directions; drain. Rinse in cold water; drain well. Spread noodles in single layer on several thicknesses of paper toweling; let dry about 4 hours. Fry noodles, a handful at a time, in deep hot fat (365°) for 2 to 3 minutes or till golden brown; drain noodles on paper toweling.

In large saucepan or Dutch oven combine water and salt; bring to boiling. Cook fried noodles in the boiling salted water for 1 minute. Drain well; serve warm with the desired main dish. Makes 6 to 8 servings.

Soft-Fried Noodles

2 **cups fine noodles**
2 **tablespoons cooking oil**
¼ **cup sliced green onion**

Cook noodles according to package directions; drain. Rinse in cold water. Drain well. Preheat wok or large skillet over high heat; add cooking oil. Stir-fry green onion in hot oil for 1 minute; add noodles and stir-fry for 5 to 7 minutes or till just beginning to brown. Serve warm with desired main dish. Makes 4 to 6 servings.

Rice

Rice is such an important staple in the Orient that the phrase "breaking your rice bowl" refers to losing your job. Every Oriental meal includes rice in what most Americans would consider large quantities (at least 1 cup cooked rice per person). When eating an Oriental meal that features several main dishes, take a few bites of rice to clear your palate before tasting a different dish. Cook rice according to package directions, or try the "no-watch" Oven Rice.

Because rice is used so extensively, it's quite common to have some left over. The Chinese have developed a delicious way to use leftover rice in fried rice. This dish is perfect for experimenting, so be creative with the basic recipe by adding ham, Oven Barbecued Pork (see recipe, page 75), cooked beef, mixed vegetables, or whatever you have on hand.

Oven Rice

1 tablespoon butter *or* margarine
2¼ cups boiling water
1 cup long grain rice
1 teaspoon salt

In 1½-quart casserole stir butter into water till melted. Stir in rice and salt. Cover; bake in 350° oven about 35 minutes or till rice is tender. Fluff with fork after 15 minutes. Makes 8 servings.

Chinese Fried Rice (pictured above)

2 beaten eggs
3 tablespoons cooking oil
½ cup finely diced fully cooked ham *or* raw pork
¼ cup finely chopped fresh mushrooms
3 tablespoons soy sauce
3 tablespoons thinly sliced green onion
4 cups cooked rice
Soy sauce

In a 10-inch skillet cook beaten eggs in *1 tablespoon* of the oil, without stirring, till set. Invert skillet over a baking sheet to remove cooked eggs; cut into short, narrow strips. In the same skillet cook ham or pork, mushrooms, 3 tablespoons soy sauce, and green onion in remaining oil about 4 minutes or till mushrooms and onion are tender. Stir in cooked rice and egg strips; heat through. Serve with additional soy sauce. Garnish with fried egg strips and sliced mushrooms, if desired. Makes 4 to 6 servings.

Sizzling Rice Soup

¼ **cup short grain rice**
1 **6-ounce package frozen pea pods**
5 **cups Homemade Chicken Broth (see recipe, page 54)**
1 **cup cooked shrimp, halved lengthwise**
½ **cup chopped bok choy**
¼ **cup sliced water chestnuts Cooking oil for deep-fat frying**
2 **tablespoons sliced green onion**

Cook rice according to package directions; cool. Divide rice into eight portions. With hands, shape and press each portion into a 2-inch patty. Thaw pea pods by running hot water over them; cut pea pods into 1-inch lengths. In saucepan heat chicken broth to boiling. Add pea pods, shrimp, bok choy, and water chestnuts; simmer 2 minutes. Reduce heat and keep warm.

Fry rice patties, four at a time, in deep hot fat (375°) about 4 minutes or till crispy and golden. Place fried rice on baking sheet and immediately put in 350° oven to keep hot while frying remaining rice.

Working quickly, place all the fried rice patties in large serving bowl and pour chicken broth mixture over (speed is important to obtain the desired sizzling.) Top with sliced green onion. Makes 8 servings.

Sushi with Smoked Fish *Japanese*

1½ **cups long, medium, *or* short grain rice**
¼ **cup rice vinegar *or* white vinegar**
¼ **cup sugar**
2 **tablespoons mirin, sake, *or* dry sherry**
½ **medium cucumber, thinly sliced**
½ **pound smoked salmon *or* other smoked fish, thinly sliced**

Cook rice according to package directions. In small saucepan combine vinegar, sugar, and mirin, sake, or dry sherry; bring to boil. Stir vinegar mixture into cooked rice; let rice mixture cool slightly.

Line 8x8x2-inch pan with waxed paper. Arrange enough of the cucumber slices to form a single layer in bottom of pan, overlapping slightly. Carefully spread *half* the rice mixture over cucumber. Arrange smoked fish atop rice in pan. Spread remaining rice atop fish. Cover with waxed paper. Place a second 8x8x2-inch pan atop and *press very firmly* to compact mixture. Remove top pan. Chill several hours. Remove top waxed paper and invert rice-salmon-cucumber mixture onto serving plate. (If rice falls apart, repeat the pressing procedure.) Remove remaining waxed paper. Cut into pieces to serve. Makes 9 appetizer servings.

Fried Rice with Shrimp

2 **beaten eggs**
⅓ **cup soy sauce**
2 **tablespoons dry sherry**
⅛ **teaspoon pepper**
2 **tablespoons cooking oil**
1 **clove garlic, minced**
1 **teaspoon grated gingerroot**
¼ **cup chopped onion**
3 **cups cooked rice**
1 **cup cooked shrimp, halved lengthwise**
1 **cup cooked *or* canned peas**

In small mixing bowl combine beaten eggs, soy sauce, dry sherry, and pepper; set aside. Preheat wok or large skillet over high heat; add cooking oil. Stir-fry garlic and gingerroot in hot oil for 30 seconds. Add chopped onion; stir-fry about 1 minute or till crisp-tender. Stir in cooked rice, shrimp, and peas. Cook, stirring frequently, for 6 to 8 minutes. While stirring constantly, drizzle egg mixture over rice. Cook, stirring constantly, till eggs are set. Makes 4 to 6 servings.

Sauces

Enhance the flavor of fried wontons and egg rolls by dunking them in tangy Sweet and Sour Sauce or Horseradish-Mustard Sauce. The pleasant fruity taste of Plum Sauce brings out the natural flavors of grilled or roasted duck and pork. And Sweet and Pungent Sauce adds a special zing when spooned over deep-fried spareribs. Simmered food, such as in firepot cooking, comes to life when served with Chinese Mustard, Ginger Soy, or Oyster Sauce. Use Oyster Sauce, too, as an ingredient to enrich stir-fried recipes.

But don't limit yourself to these suggestions. Experiment! Try these sauces with many different foods, and savor your own flavor combinations. When you're in a rush and don't have the time to make your own sauces, you can purchase most of them at large supermarkets or Oriental specialty shops. Pictured above: Horseradish-Mustard Sauce, Ginger Soy, Sweet and Sour Sauce, Plum Sauce, and Chinese Mustard.

Sweet and Pungent Sauce

1 small green pepper
1 8¼-ounce can pineapple chunks
2 tablespoons brown sugar
4 teaspoons cornstarch
1 8-ounce can tomatoes, cut up
¼ cup finely chopped onion
1 tablespoon vinegar
1 tablespoon soy sauce

Cut green pepper in 1-inch squares. Drain pineapple, reserving ⅓ cup syrup. Combine reserved syrup, brown sugar, cornstarch, and ⅛ teaspoon *salt*. Stir in *undrained* tomatoes, onion, vinegar, and soy sauce. Cook and stir till bubbly. Stir in pineapple and green pepper. Heat through. (Use with Sweet and Pungent Spareribs, page 31.) Makes 2½ cups.

Serving suggestion: Substitute crushed pineapple and chopped green pepper when serving with wontons and egg rolls.

Horseradish-Mustard Sauce

1 tablespoon butter *or* margarine
2 tablespoons dijon-style mustard
1 tablespoon all-purpose flour
1 tablespoon prepared horseradish
  Several drops bottled hot pepper sauce
½ cup Homemade Chicken Broth (see recipe, page 54)
½ cup light cream *or* milk
2 teaspoons snipped chives
1 teaspoon lemon juice

In a small saucepan melt butter or margarine; blend in mustard, flour, horseradish, bottled hot pepper sauce, ¼ teaspoon *salt,* and dash *pepper*. Add chicken broth and light cream or milk. Cook and stir till mixture is bubbly. Remove from heat; stir in snipped chives and lemon juice. Serve warm. Makes 1¼ cups.

Plum Sauce

1 **12-ounce jar plum preserves**
2 **tablespoons vinegar**
1 **tablespoon brown sugar**
1 **tablespoon finely chopped onion**
1 **teaspoon seeded and finely chopped dried red chili pepper *or* 1 teaspoon crushed red pepper**
1 **clove garlic, minced**
½ **teaspoon ground ginger**

In a small saucepan combine plum preserves, vinegar, brown sugar, onion, red chili pepper or crushed red pepper, garlic, and ground ginger. Bring mixture to boiling, stirring constantly. Remove from heat; cool slightly. Refrigerate in a covered container overnight to blend seasonings. Makes 1¼ cups.

Chinese Mustard

¼ **cup water**
¼ **cup dry mustard**
2 **teaspoons cooking oil**
½ **teaspoon salt**

In small saucepan bring water to boiling. Combine dry mustard, cooking oil, and salt. Stir boiling water into mustard mixture. Makes about ⅓ cup sauce.

Sweet and Sour Sauce

½ **cup packed brown sugar**
1 **tablespoon cornstarch**
⅓ **cup red wine vinegar**
⅓ **cup Homemade Chicken Broth (see recipe, page 54)**
¼ **cup finely chopped green pepper**
2 **tablespoons chopped pimiento**
1 **tablespoon soy sauce**
¼ **teaspoon garlic powder**
¼ **teaspoon ground ginger**

In a small saucepan combine brown sugar and cornstarch. Stir in the red wine vinegar, chicken broth, green pepper, pimiento, soy sauce, garlic powder, and ground ginger. Cook and stir till thick and bubbly. Serve warm. Makes 1¼ cups sauce.

Oyster Sauce

1 **pint shucked oysters**
Water
¼ **cup soy sauce**
Few drops kitchen bouquet (optional)

Drain oysters, reserving liquid. Add enough water to reserved liquid to measure 1 cup. In saucepan combine oysters, the 1 cup liquid, soy sauce, and kitchen bouquet, if desired. Cook, stirring constantly, about 5 minutes or till oysters curl. Cool. Pour half of the mixture into a blender container. Cover and blend till smooth; remove from blender. Repeat with remaining mixture. Pour sauce into jar with a screw-top lid. Store, covered, in the refrigerator (keeps for several weeks). Makes 2⅓ cups.

Ginger Soy

½ **cup soy sauce**
¼ **cup water**
1½ **teaspoons ground ginger**

In saucepan combine soy sauce, water, and ginger. Heat through. Serve warm. Makes ¾ cup sauce.

Desserts

Desserts, as we know them in our Western culture, aren't traditional with Oriental menus. In the Orient, very sweet desserts are not normally a part of everyday family meals, but are customarily eaten as a snack at teatime or for special occasions. For an interesting tidbit of sweetness, you can serve a piece of candied or preserved ginger, preserved kumquats, or cookies. An easy-to-fix fruit compote such as Almond Cubes with Fruit or Chilled Fruit Toss is a welcome finale after a spicy hot dinner. And fresh or canned fruit is a traditional and most appreciated finish to an Oriental meal. Tangerines, nectarines, oranges, grapes, peaches, cherries, apples, pears, melons, and persimmons are all favored for their lightness and mild sweetness.

Orientals particularly enjoy strawberries, watermelon, or fresh pineapple chilled and served in its shell. Prepare pineapple by rinsing, then twist off the crown and cut off the base. Cut the pineapple in quarters lengthwise and cut out the hard core. Starting from one end, cut the fruit from the peel, leaving pineapple in its shell. All that's left is to slice crosswise into bite-size pieces. For a special touch you can garnish with fresh mint. This is a spectacular dessert, which is refreshing, easy, and completely authentic.

Fortune Cookies

¼ cup sifted cake flour
2 tablespoons sugar
1 tablespoon cornstarch
   Dash salt
2 tablespoons cooking oil
1 egg white
1 tablespoon water

Sift together flour, sugar, cornstarch, and salt. Add oil and egg white; stir till smooth. Add the water; mix well. Make one cookie at a time by pouring 1 tablespoonful of the batter on lightly greased skillet or griddle; spread to 3½-inch circle. Cook over low heat about 4 minutes or till lightly browned. Turn with wide spatula; cook 1 minute more. Working quickly, place cookie on pot holder. Put paper strip printed with fortune in center; fold cookie in half and then fold again over edge of bowl (see tip on page 87). Place in muffin pan to cool. Makes 8.

Preparation tip: Before you start making the cookies, write fortunes with predictions of good health, prosperity, and/or happiness on small strips of paper for enclosing in the cookies as instructed above.